D0998677

Praise for *The Sinking of RMS* Tayleur

'A fascinating, well-researched account of this memorial shipwreck, one of the worst in Ireland's history. Highly recommended'.
Richard Larn OBE, author of *Lloyd's Shipwreck Index of Ireland and Great Britain*

'A first class voyage of discovery. Gill Hoffs delivers a detailed and vivid account of the shameful loss of the *Tayleur* and the inadequate inquiry, in this skilful post-mortem of Victorian sea-going values'.
Dr Ronnie Scott, Centre for Open Studies, University of Glasgow

'This well-written and thoroughly researched book takes us inside a deadly shipwreck, and presents that tragedy in the larger context of Victorian life. Gill Hoffs has given us a compelling, heart-rending read. The sinking of RMS *Tayleur* is lost no more'.
Gregory Gibson, author of *Demon of the Waters: The True Story of the Mutiny of the Whaleship Globe*

'Gill Hoffs' maiden voyage as a major nautical-historical author comes off wonderfully. The violent death of the RMS *Tayleur* is both a heartbreaking and horrifying story, competently and clearly told. Hoffs manages to set the historical Victorian tone and mood just right.

'Masterfully, she weaves in the stories of the many passengers so that we never lose sight of the human in the disaster. We see the desperation of the famine Irish and the other 'down and out' passengers. We share in their hopes and dreams of being rich on Australian gold. Then, when disaster strikes on the Irish coast, we see ourselves reflected in the victims as they fight to survive a cruel and angry ocean.

'Making liberal use of first person accounts, the book is a vivid and frightening elegy that should appeal to many readers'.
Marc Songini, author of *The Lost Fleet*

'In the flood of shipwreck narratives regularly published, *The Sinking of RMS* Tayleur is a rare and unusual find. Unusual, because the calamity, horrific as it was, has been virtually forgotten. Rare, because the author sets the time and place so carefully, focusing on the desperation of the poor emigrants bound for a new life in Australia...

'Hoffs switches skilfully between two points of view: an omniscient wide-angle lens that zooms out and with precise language allows us to watch everything unfold in all its chilling fascination; and the close-up, where amongst the chaos we watch doomed tableaux of heroism and cowardice, panic and a strange, determined calm.

'When one considers Hoffs' observation that hundreds of ships sank monthly, taking with them thousands of unlucky souls, one wonders why anyone went anywhere by ship. The answer, of course, is simple – they had no other choice ... heartbreaking and humbling'.
Joe Jackson, author of *Atlantic Fever*

Praise for Gill Hoffs' previous work, *Wild* (published by Pure Slush)

'*Wild* offers exceptional fiction and reportage, with a coast-dweller's sharp eye for maritime detail, and a humane regard for both the victims and the survivors of shipwrecks, both literal and metaphorical. From *Prospects*, a marvellous, moving reconstruction of the murderous maiden voyage of the *Tayleur*, to *Luck is in the Leftovers*, a gripping saga of living on the edge of the land, where life and death ebb and flow like the tides, Gill Hoffs' writing, fiction and non, swells with the power of life, sometimes life at the expense of other lives, but always animated and alive. This is visceral and vital prose, smooth as a sea-worn pebble yet sharp as sharks' teeth'.
Ronnie Scott, author of *Death by Design* and editor of *Tommy's War*, *Tommy's Peace* and *The Real 'Dads' Army'*

'In her tales, Gill Hoffs' unique voice has tamed the wild creating narratives of raw beauty. When I put the book down, I could taste the salt of the green sea on my tongue'.
Marcus Speh, author of *Thank You For Your Sperm*

'A collection of short stories and non-fiction that brings the reader to the sea, to wild Scotland. Hoffs' prose is salty, rocky and storm-blown: a right and memorable voice that grabs the reader and does not let go'.
Christopher Allen, author of *Conversations with S. Teri O'Type*

The Sinking of
RMS *Tayleur*

Dedicated to:
my Aunt Jean and Uncle Jim, who got me interested in shipwrecks;
my husband and son, who keep me whole;
and all those affected by struggles won and lost at sea.

The Sinking of RMS *Tayleur*

The Lost Story of the 'Victorian *Titanic*'

Gill Hoffs

PEN & SWORD
HISTORY

First published in Great Britain in 2014 by
Pen & Sword History
an imprint of
Pen & Sword Books Ltd
47 Church Street
Barnsley
South Yorkshire
S70 2AS

Copyright © Gill Hoffs 2014

ISBN 978 1 78303 047 7

The right of Gill Hoffs to be identified as the Author of this Work has
been asserted by her in accordance with the Copyright, Designs and
Patents Act 1988.

A CIP catalogue record for this book is available from the British
Library.

All rights reserved. No part of this book may be reproduced or
transmitted in any form or by any means, electronic or mechanical
including photocopying, recording or by any information storage and
retrieval system, without permission from the Publisher in writing.

Typeset in Ehrhardt by
Mac Style, Bridlington, East Yorkshire
Printed and bound in the UK by CPI Group (UK) Ltd, Croydon,
CRO 4YY

Pen & Sword Books Ltd incorporates the imprints of Pen & Sword
Archaeology, Atlas, Aviation, Battleground, Discovery, Family History,
History, Maritime, Military, Naval, Politics, Railways, Select,
Social History, Transport, True Crime, and Claymore Press,
Frontline Books, Leo Cooper, Praetorian Press, Remember When,
Seaforth Publishing and Wharncliffe.

For a complete list of Pen & Sword titles please contact
PEN & SWORD BOOKS LIMITED
47 Church Street, Barnsley, South Yorkshire, S70 2AS, England
E-mail: enquiries@pen-and-sword.co.uk
Website: www.pen-and-sword.co.uk

Contents

... being in a ship is being in a jail, with a chance of being drowned
Samuel Johnson, in a letter to Tobias Smollet, 1759

Liverpool, 4 January 1854
My Dear and Affectionate Wife—I hope to God this will find you well and
comfortable. I arrived here at 5 o'clock yesterday. I have embarked on board
the Tayleur, *at 12 o'clock this day, in the greatest confusion. We are 600*
passengers now on board, and I write on the crown of my hat. I shall live in
hopes of seeing you again, my dear woman.
I am, yours till death,
Thomas W. Lloyd.

Preface

I had never heard of the RMS *Tayleur* until a visit to Warrington Museum a few years ago. Amidst the more exotic exhibits of mummies, cannibal cutlery and shrunken heads, nestled a small display of chipped crockery, and a brass porthole with a few barnacles still clinging to the glass. One of the curators saw me pause by the old plates, and explained that a shipwreck over 150 years ago had led to these artefacts being deposited there. He advised me to read the survivors' accounts of the disaster. I sobbed when I did.

When the wreck occurred 70 children were travelling with their families on the ship to Australia. My son was a toddler at the time of our visit, and I could picture the adults on board clutching their terrified children and howling for help as ropes snapped and planks fell. Others lay in their bunks tortured with seasickness as the water flooded over them. It was horrible, but very similar to a thousand other shipwrecks during the nineteenth century. What really hit me, however, was the demographic of the people involved. So few women and children were saved, yet the ship had been positioned so close to safety that 'between life and death there intervened only a space that passengers traverse daily in walking from a steamer's dock to the pier', as the *Leeds Times* remarked. I wondered why so many had died. The story had taken root in my mind, and I knew the only way to exorcise it was to uncover the fates of the travellers and crew, then commit them to paper.

In early 2012 I wrote a short non-fiction piece called 'Fairer Prospects' (included in *Wild: a collection*, published by Pure Slush) on the *Tayleur* and one of her most intriguing survivors: an anonymous baby dubbed 'The Ocean Child' by the Victorian press, who was found lying alone on the deck of the sinking ship. The more research I did into the disaster the more questions I had (many of which are answered in this book). I became obsessed with learning whatever I could about the wreck and those involved with the ship. Who was the Ocean Child, and what happened to him? What was the real story behind the ex-convict passenger who had struck it rich in the Australian Gold Rush and returned to England with a fortune? Who was the mysterious 'Mr Jones' and what were his motives for attempting to deceive the inquest? And *why* did this brand new ship with her able captain wreck in the first place?

Other books on the *Tayleur*, including Edward Bourke's incredibly useful *Bound For Australia* (self-published, 2003) and Bert Starkey's *Iron Clipper* (Avid Publications, 1999), focus mainly on the ship, the problems with the compasses, and other practical matters leading to the accident. These issues have been examined repeatedly by people with the technical knowledge to do them justice. As a non-sailor and psychology graduate, I came at the wreck from a different angle. I wanted to know more about the individuals on board. What had driven or enticed them to travel overseas at a time when drunken captains, maggoty bread, monster rats, thick, green, algae-clogged drinking water and death at sea were commonplace? Why did so many women and children drown on the *Tayleur* or have their heads 'stove in', as one survivor put it, on the rocks while swimming to safety? What might have happened to the captain that could account for his mistakes leading up to the wreck, and why were certain key questions never asked in the aftermath?

* * *

When writing about events that occurred so long ago – and events that were reported at a time of great prejudice – inevitably some inaccuracies will creep in. Some of the accounts of the wreck are contradictory, and the exact number of people who travelled on the *Tayleur* is unlikely to ever be known for definite. Whenever I encountered conflicting information I sought help from experts or knowledgeable friends, made educated guesses and highlighted gaps or inconclusive evidence in the narrative. Where appropriate, I chose to let these long-dead Victorians speak for themselves and I have tried not to shy away from their more shocking statements, nor have I applied modern values to nineteenth century sentiments and beliefs. When the *Tayleur* sank, the Crimean War was in its early stages, children were expendable, executions were carried out in public, and the Beard And Moustache Movement promoted the growing of facial hair by the working classes – this is the world that I've attempted to give a sense of in this book.

I read thousands of Victorian newspaper articles during my research, and found them to be at times grisly, pompous, silly and sentimental, but always utterly fascinating. Journalists reveal nineteenth century society as its inhabitants saw it, and the parallels between then and now are striking. Concerns about work, education, healthcare and marriage prospects abound. The people who travelled on the *Tayleur* wanted to build secure futures for themselves and their loved ones. They took a risk that did not pay off, and many lost their lives in the process.

The disaster also tainted the lives of those involved in the running of the *Tayleur*. The White Star Line suffered a significant setback over the tragedy, from the physical loss of the under-insured ship as well as the damage to their image. It was eventually declared bankrupt in 1867, when the Royal Bank of Liverpool, which had backed the shipping company, went bust, leaving the White Star Line with massive debts. Its ships and associated goods were dispersed, and in 1868 the name, branding and goodwill were sold to Thomas Henry 'Baccy' Ismay, the tobacco-chewing founder of the Ocean Steam Navigation Company (from then on renamed the White Star Line). His son, J. Bruce Ismay, later took over the company and survived the sinking of the RMS *Titanic* in 1912.

As Starkey and Bourke have previously noted, the fate of the *Tayleur* is eerily similar to that of the infamous *Titanic*, which also sank on its maiden voyage 58 years later. Both were enormous metal ships which sank in unusual circumstances on their maiden voyages, and both had been celebrated in the press as heralding a new era of luxury for travellers. Both collisions would likely have had significantly lower death tolls had the vessels hit the obstacles head-on instead of sideswiping them. Both tragedies led to better legislation and safer journeys for the hundreds of thousands who crossed oceans in search of a happier life or an escape from their old one. This book is primarily a tale about the passengers and crew on the *Tayleur*, focusing on their short, deadly voyage and its suspiciously-handled aftermath, but the comparisons between the two ships are unnerving.

The *Tayleur* was one of 893 vessels known to have wrecked in the waters around Great Britain and Ireland in 1854. Official records quoted in the periodical *Life-boat* note a death toll of 1,549 that year, but a lot more may have perished, as records were inexact and stowaways were common. With an average of two or three ships wrecking every day, it might have been easy to grow hardened to the deaths of travellers and crewmen. Yet as *Life-boat* reminded its readers, 'one human life is as valuable as another, at least to its possessor; and the poor emigrant, or other wayfarer of the sea, may leave as long a train of sorrowing relatives and friends to mourn his loss as any other individual'.

Hundreds of those leaving the port of Liverpool on the *Tayleur* in January 1854 would not make it off the fancy new ship alive, but many did, and their survival was thrilling to research. Contacting their descendants felt very odd, as it made the deaths of their ancestors' fellow travellers even more real to me. It was a satisfying, though unsettling sensation, and something I bore in mind while I wrote about their last moments. I clung to the examples of heroism and selflessness displayed by some of the people involved in the wreck and its aftermath, while writing of the cover-ups and villainy that dogged the *Tayleur*'s brief existence.

Here is their story.

Gill Hoffs,
Warrington, 2 June 2013

Chapter One

Whoever comes to this part of Australia, with strong limbs and a stout heart, determined to do his part in the busy hive, will be sure of a rich reward. He cannot fail to prosper. Drones had better stay at home. There is no room for them in this land of business. They will find neither resources nor sympathy.

There is no royal road even to Australian gold. Like knowledge, it can be reached only by earnest and persevering toil. Like knowledge, too, it is certain to be found by those who seek it aright. If not found at the mines, it may be found elsewhere. If not found in the shape of nuggets, the hard-working man will always find it in the shape of excellent wages. We repeat, therefore, let all who cannot or will not work remain where they are, since there is nothing here worth their coming for; let all who can and will work lose no time in joining us, for there is here everything to cheer and prosper them.

(*Elgin Courier*, 29 July 1853)

Victorian Britain was a strange cultural mix of glory and guilt, prim delicacy and delight in the macabre. The world was changing at a frightening rate and many Britons sought to exploit new opportunities promising adventure and escape. The year 1853 was a time of industrial development and discovery, yet slaves were still bought and sold in America, child sweeps thrust up chimneys, and newspapers reported incidents of witchcraft as fact. It was the year that Queen Victoria gave birth to her eighth child, Prince Leopold; a time of knowledge and superstition, when the joy of creativity and discovery proved a useful distraction for the better-off from the misery of the masses.

The Victorian state provided no safety net for the sick, aged or poor. As the *Taunton Courier* reported in 1848, children in London described as the 'wretched dregs' of society endured hard lives in prison, on the street, or sometimes in lodging houses seen as 'nests of every abomination'. Many were without shoes, hats or undergarments to keep them warm. Some had never slept in a bed. City streets were crowded with homeless people 'in the habit of passing the night under dry arches of bridges and viaducts, under porticoes, sheds, carts, sawpits, staircases, wherever shelter could be found and intrusion avoided'. The situation was growing increasingly dire in the provinces as well as the crowded cities, with more than one in 17 people in England and Wales classed as a pauper by an 1848 Poor Law Board report.

Officially, a pauper was someone in receipt of poor relief, for example, food, clothing or shelter, either in the workhouse or within the wider community. Many people would rather die than suffer the shame of the workhouse; entering one also meant isolation and separation from their spouse and children. One man, who 'had lately complained of being reduced to poverty on account of the bad times', cut his throat in a pub in Blackburn, according to the suicides section of the *Liverpool Mercury* in 1847. This was not an uncommon response. The 1840s were a terrible time for the vulnerable and impoverished, with almost a million paupers in England and Wales claiming relief of some description in 1849, after a catastrophically poor harvest across Europe.

In 1845 the potato famine began in Ireland, sparking years of misery and resulting in the emigration of thousands. In the mid-1800s Ireland was dependent on the potato crop, both for sustenance and animal fodder. Fields were used to raise crops and animals for export, leaving little but potatoes to feed the working class. When blight struck in the early 1840s, first in America, then spreading across Europe, the fields yielded a rotten grey sludge that led to starvation, death and disease for over a million people within just five years. The decade became known as the 'Hungry Forties', meanwhile landowners in Ireland continued to export shiploads of corn and cattle; to some it was not truly a 'famine', it was 'starvation'. George Bernard Shaw commented in his 1903 play *Man and Superman*, 'when a country is full of food, and exporting it, there can be no famine'.

The living lay beside the dead, too weak to bury the corpses or even to lay them outside. The newspapers were full of graphic accounts and attempts to elicit donations to workhouses overwhelmed by the influx of starving people;

hundreds were turned away to die outside in the open air. 'I shall never forget the impression made on my mind a few days ago by a most heart-rending case of starvation', the Reverend Fitzgerald of Kilgeever, County Mayo, Ireland, told the *Devizes and Wiltshire Gazette* in 1847:

> *I have witnessed [a] poor mother of five sending her little children, almost lifeless from hunger, to bed, and, despairing of ever seeing them again alive, she took her last leave of them. In the morning, her first act was to touch their lips with her hand to see if the breath of life still remained: but the poor mother's fears were not groundless, for not a breath could she feel from some of her dear little children; that night [she had] buried them in the night of eternity.*

Two years later the same paper included a report from another clergyman, Reverend Osborne, on the situation in Ireland. Osborne had encountered groups of emaciated families on the road in search of food:

> *There were donkeys looking decently fed, thistles abound; on the sides of these animals they hang the turf panniers, and in these they put the very young children; it looked as if skeletons had bred in wicker baskets. Some way behind one of these travelling groups of Lazari [after Lazarus who was raised from the dead by Jesus in the Bible] there was a boy of about 12 riding a donkey; he looked within a week of the grave; he could not kick his steed, for his feet were blue and frightfully swollen; he had no strength to strike so as to be felt, with his shrunken hands and arms; a donkey for once was master of a boy.*

Some assistance was given by the British Government in the form of shiploads of provisions, accompanied by men willing to distribute it to the needy. 'Fever, dysentery, and starvation, stare you in the face everywhere', one sailor told the *Bath Chronicle and Weekly Gazette* in 1847. 'Babes are found lifeless, lying on their mothers' bosoms. I will tell you one thing which struck me as peculiarly horrible; a dead woman was found lying on the road with a dead infant on her breast, the child having bitten the nipple of the mother's breast right through in trying to derive nourishment from the wretched body. Dogs feed on the half-buried dead, and rats are commonly known to tear people to pieces, who, though still alive, are too weak to cry out'.

For many, assistance came too late or not at all. People continued to weaken and die as the stench of rotting bodies and vegetation filled the land. The Public Record Office of Northern Ireland estimates that between 1845 and 1850, around 800,000 Irish people died of starvation and related diseases, such as dysentery, scurvy and typhus.

Emigration seemed the perfect escape and many Irish people fled to England via Liverpool. Large families crowded into squalid rooms in boarding-houses and lodgings there, sharing accommodation meant for far fewer people, and desperate for food, water, and the money to go elsewhere. The *Newcastle Guardian and Tyne Mercury* reported in 1863 that during the Irish Potato Famine:

> *Lancashire experienced a death rate which looked as though she herself were stricken with pestilence. In 1846 and 1847 provisions, in consequence of the failure of the potato, were dear, and employment scarce from the depression of trade. The starving Irish thronged the quays of Liverpool, and crowded the streets of Manchester; or they were huddled together beyond all experience, in the poorest and dirtiest of neighbourhoods. "Liverpool," said the Registrar-General, "has for a year been the hospital and cemetery of Ireland".*

Those who didn't succumb to disease continued their journeys to Scotland, Canada and America. In some of the countries receiving starving Irish families, particularly England, the rich muttered about overcrowding, the poor about competition for jobs. The middle classes felt the pressure too; unlike the rich, they were not cushioned by wealth and social position, yet unlike the poor, they might have enough money to do something about it, perhaps even leaving the country in search of a more comfortable life.

In 1854 one gentleman praised emigration in a letter to the *Devizes & Wiltshire Gazette*. He explained that he had received a letter appealing to him to urge more healthy emigrants to depart for Australia as soon as possible, especially women:

I think it would be wise to comply as relates to sending out some more females, as it is very desirable that there should be a great preponderance of the Saxon blood. No doubt Australia will be a great and powerful country another day, and if properly managed in its infancy, may be a useful ally, &c., to England some years hence; but as I read that there are Irish, Chinese, and perhaps Esquimaux, &c., &c., there already, the future population will be a mixed medley indeed.

So far as the labour market is concerned in this little hamlet (only a small part of the parish), we can still readily spare 6 adults of each sex, without being missed or enquired for, except at the beer-houses and to pay their debts at the shops; but I hear of no one wishing to go in this large and thickly-populated parish – they don't like the water. And as to children, they swarm like bees on a fine day; how they are packed together at night will not bear inspection. In Scripture we are told to increase and multiply and populate the EARTH: we have done the two first, and we are now killing each other by overcrowding diseases; and as no one seems to like building cottages, elbow room and opportunities to populate the earth seem to be much desired.

The British Government had already taken up the idea of emigration and paid for shiploads of paupers to sail to Australia, including children, young women and able men. In 1850, Parliament agreed that Poor Law Guardians could, with the local Poor Law Board's consent, pay for the children in their care to emigrate. It seemed to offer them a fresh start and, perhaps more significantly, was also cheaper than paying for their upkeep. British children had been sent abroad by the government since 1619, when 100 vagrant children were shipped to newly-settled Virginia to augment the workforce there. This cannot have been an enviable fate. Another shipload arrived a few years later to help restock a settlement, after its inhabitants had been killed in a retaliatory attack by the Powhatan Confederacy, a group of American Indians living in the area.

Pauper children were an expensive problem for the authorities of the time, and were often used as cheap labour. As a report from the *Freeman's Journal* in 1850 indicates, the great and good did not conceive of these children as individuals: 'They had been of late years sending female pauper children to Australia, and they had heard good and bad reports as to their reception there ... [at a meeting held in Sydney] some were in favour of having Irish pauper girls sent out there, while others were for these from England and Scotland, as being the best educated, and best adapted for agricultural business'.

The Board of Guardians in Cork summed up what many of the upper classes believed at the time, when they discussed the transportation of workhouse children in 1848: 'Those unfortunate creatures if not removed at an early age, would crowd the jails and inevitably be transported at a maturer age, at a great expense to the country'. These learned gentlemen also remarked that it would be 'better to send them at infinitely less cost to Australia, where they would have an opportunity of earning an honest livelihood'.

Children, convicts and the healthier poor would often have their passage paid by the government, with pauper women sometimes offered gold chains and crosses to relocate overseas and become 'virtuous wives, and happy mothers'. The *Hereford Journal* considered the sending of young girls and women to Australia to redress the gender imbalance 'natural and humane', remarking that 'the domestic services of a wife are invaluable. The rustle of a petticoat awakens the most tender interest'. The newspaper encouraged women to consider the benefits of immigration 'to the comforts of a sheltered home'.

However, most adults seeking a fresh start and a chance of better fortune had to find the money for the tickets, the fare to the docks, luggage, and provisions on board. Some men worked their passage, receiving bed and board and a nominal fee in return for acting as stewards or seamen on the ship. Captains' names were advertised alongside the details of their vessels to tempt passengers and crew to sign up. Captain John Noble, of Penrith, was popular for his record-breaking trip from Liverpool to Australia, then on to Amoy (via the West Indies and New Orleans) before sailing swiftly back to Liverpool in just over 13 months. He was also praised for the healthy environment he maintained on his ship throughout the trip.

Yet not all descriptions of captains' virtues were as accurate. Some were notorious drunks who ran sloppy ships and had high mortality rates among their passengers. Others brought ill fortune to those who sailed with them, like Captain Timothy Stinson, who was known for abandoning his passengers when the *William and Mary* was wrecked off the Bahamas in 1853. Stinson's crew had chopped at the desperate survivors with a hatchet to prevent passengers from climbing into lifeboats packed with food and valuable cargo. They left two dead in shark-infested waters. Luckily for the other 180 abandoned on the grounded vessel, two plucky sailors chose to stay with them until another ship saved them from their plight three days later. Stinson was briefly castigated in the newspapers, but no charges appear to have been pressed against him and the 31-year-old American slunk home to live out his remaining decades on dry land.

While cases like this may have deterred some Britons from travelling overseas, at the time there was still an insatiable thirst for adventure and the chance to start afresh. Some would-be emigrants took desperate measures. In 1852 a Derby man called Charles Robinson set fire to a hayrick in Stratford-on-Avon simply because he was 'wishing to be transported', or so the *Stamford Mercury* reported.

Transportation of convicts to Australia and nearby Tasmania helped to alleviate the severe over-crowding in British prisons. Convicts had been shipped to Australia since 1787, and to America and sometimes the West Indies since the early 1600s. Australia became the preferred option when the start of the American Revolutionary War in 1776 made it too dangerous, and then once America achieved independence it rejected any further shiploads of British convicts.

Though some convicts were sentenced to transportation to the British colonies for serious offences, such as murder and assault, many more were sent abroad for trivial crimes, such as stealing a loaf of bread or an animal. Samuel Carby, aged 22, had already served one month in Exeter Gaol for stealing a horse in 1841, when a few months after his release he was prosecuted for stealing a chunk of flesh from a single sheep. Along with an older accomplice, ploughman George Bell, Carby was sentenced to ten years' transportation – equivalent to the term some murderers received. After they departed on the ship that would carry them halfway round the world, detailed descriptions of each convict were logged in a large brown book. Should any man escape, or claim another prisoner's identity and sentence as his own, the authorities aimed to record enough detail in the book to discover him.

Samuel Carby's record reads:

Height without shoes, 5 ft 4; age, 23; Complexion, fresh; Head, large; Hair, dark brown; Whiskers, none; Visage, oval; Forehead, MHt [medium height]; Eyebrows, black; Eyes, hazel; Nose, long; Mouth, medium; Chin, large; Remarks, scar on right breast, large scar near right elbow, 2 scars on left arm, scar under left eye.

Compared to some of the more careworn prisoners, like the 'pock-pitted', large-nostrilled, 'hairy', stoutly built Samuel Beard, who was also aboard the *Gilmore* and for some reason had a 'blue scar over [his] left eye', Carby sounds positively handsome.

His partner-in-crime, George Bell, was described as 5 ft 6 inches without shoes, clean shaven and ruddy-faced, with brown hair and a blue speck in the iris of his right eye. Like Carby, he bore a few scars, but the record notes that the 28-year-old also had an anchor tattooed on his left forearm and his own initials on the back of his left hand. Both men declared themselves free of marital ties on their record, although both were fathers. Their characters and connections marked down by the authorities as 'bad', the two arrived in Van Diemen's Land (now Tasmania) on 20 August 1843. It had been a long and unpleasant voyage – 18 sweltering weeks for the 254 convicts on board.

Once in Van Diemen's Land, the worst of the convicts would have been locked up in the imposing stone gaol nicknamed 'Hell on Earth', in an unfamiliar land of snakes and spiders that could kill with a single bite, ill-tempered scorpions, and jumping ants. The better-behaved convicts were hired out to work the fields and cultivate the land, tend to livestock, and help to develop the colony. Many prisoners worked hard, hoping for a pardon that would allow them to settle in Australia or Van Diemen's Land as free men and women, seek their passage home, or try to strike it rich in the Gold Rush.

The Australian Gold Rush officially began in 1851, when an Englishman, Edward Hargraves, discovered gold at a place he named 'Ophir'. There had already been several small finds, but this heralded an influx of prospectors known as 'diggers'. After serving out his sentence, Samuel Carby, along with other freed and escaped convicts, travelled from Van Diemen's Land to the diggings, hoping to make his fortune.

The Gold Rush immigrants came from all over the world, tempted by promises of a better life, making a fortune, and increased social mobility. They were encouraged to do so by their own governments. Adverts targeting the poor had appeared in the press for several decades, such as this one published by the *Leeds Times* in 1835:

In the Australian Colonies, the climate is so delightful as to enable the out-door labourer [to] <u>work all the year round</u>. Wages are nearly double what is obtained for the same description of work in Canada. Land, <u>free of timber and ready for the plough</u>, may be bought at 5s. per acre, while the nearness of the Indian Ports offer an opening for their produce which the American settler does not possess. The coast, too, abounds with whales of the finest description, affording to the Colonists upwards of £158,000 per annum; and the climate is so favourable to the growth of sheep's wool, that upwards of twenty cargoes were brought to England last year, and sold at from 1s. to 10s. per lb.

To Combined Workmen and Overseers of Parishes the advantages of Emigration are earnestly recommended, inasmuch as the arrangements now announced enable these bodies for the cost of one year's maintenance, to be relieved for ever of the burden of their able-bodied dependants. And to the individuals sent out it must be very gratifying to remain no longer a burden on their distressed countrymen; and encouraging, in as far as it removes them to the healthiest and most prosperous Colonies, where the most destitute peasant that can be landed may, if industrious and provident, save enough out of his first year's earnings to become the possessor of fifty acres of rich Land clear of timber and ready for the plough ... In addition to every sort of farm produce, their estates will yield them abundance of Grapes, Peaches, and all European fruits, Wine, valuable Timber, Coal &c. The castor oil and the olive oil trees also abound; and sugar, tea and tobacco may likewise be cultivated. There are no taxes; living is not half so expensive as in England ... The <u>Man of Small Capital</u>, who merely vegetates at home, and who occupies a very humble station in society, may there enjoy every luxury, be looked up to – and be under no apprehension about the future independence of his family; a striking contrast to the necessity he feels at home of being obliged to spend his time and his money, actually begging for employment for his sons.

But it was a dangerous dream to pursue before vaccinations, antibiotics, effective painkillers, good hygiene and ships with sufficient lifeboats. Many captains and crew were honourable, conscientious men, but this was not always the case. As one mid-nineteenth century traveller, J.H. Barrow, reported to the *Bradford Observer* in early January 1854: 'The first part of our voyage passed off tolerably pleasant; but when we reached the tropics, fever broke out, and scarcely a person escaped. All the children on board were very ill; some most dangerously; but only *one* died. After the fever was subdued, various cutaneous [skin] diseases broke out; and when the medical inspector boarded us off Adelaide, he ordered the beds and bedding to be burnt'.

Barrow was unfortunate to have been travelling to Australia on one of many ships where costs had been cut and illegal profits made by the crew at the passengers' expense. As he told the newspaper:

Our ship was greatly crowded. Instead of a maximum of 80 souls – which we were assured would be the case – there were 161. Ventilation was very defective: the conveniences both on deck and between decks, were from the first in a state of inconceivable filth; every part of the vessel reeked with bad smells, and instead of three barrels of chloride of lime, which the doctor was assured were on board, only two could be found – and when one of those was opened, it contained – chalk! Medical stores were shamefully neglected; and the doctor himself told me that of the "medical comforts" prescribed by the Act [of parliament made to protect those travelling at sea], and required to be put on board, a large number of the most important articles had been wholly omitted and of the rest only a nominal quantity had been shipped.

Our provisions were very short; the water rations were curtailed at 60 days, and subsequently further reduced; whilst salt fish, sugar, raisins, coffee, rice, preserved meats, preserved potatoes, &c., all disappeared one after the other, before our voyage was ended. As for our own family, I know not what we should have done, but for the stores I took with us. The engagement of the owner, as set forth in his prospectus, was most flagrantly broken; and the "contract ticket" was set at defiance. To crown all, we were in perpetual uproar from the drunkenness that prevailed on board, consequent upon the indiscriminate sale of ardent spirits; whilst we all along ran the greatest risk of fire, from the reckless manner in which the mates and sailors carried naked candles about in the ship's hold, amongst the loose straw which was most wickedly allowed to remain there. The second mate twice set his cabin on fire, burning all its contents to ashes.

Fire was a constant threat on board ships of the time, whether they were constructed of wood or metal. Just five years before Barrow's journey to Australia, an American packet-ship called the *Ocean Monarch* had caught fire at sea. Though surrounded by water, there was little chance of escape for the passengers and crew on board, as the *Chester Chronicle* reported in 1848:

The flames proceeded from the store-room, and extended with an extraordinary and frightful rapidity, owing in some measure to the disordered state of the steerage deck, for it generally takes a day after sailing to put things in order, and get "ship-shape". The appearance of the flames was the signal for the utmost confusion; the passengers, in their alarm and terror, rushed against each other, and greatly impeded the progress of persons getting on deck. Children were cruelly thrust aside, and women struggled in vain against some men who thought only of themselves. In the impulse of the moment, those who had money attempted to save it, and the struggle was to get on deck with trunks, boxes, clothes, &c. Many were successful, and several even returned and descended in the smoke for the purpose of saving children or getting at their little properties. But in their endeavour a great number were smothered, for a dense smoke soon filled every place below deck ... the fire having now burst upon deck, sweeping with tongues of flame ...

The persons who were on board, and happily survived the catastrophe, describe the scene at this moment as truly awful and terrific. Men, women, and children, were running about wildly, screaming and crying; a crowd got around the captain and mate, beseeching them to save them, or reproaching them for what had taken place.

Orders were either not heard or disobeyed; and the second mate and some of the crew, seeing ruin inevitable, proceeded to get out the boats, without the captain's order and against his wishes ... After the departure of the boats, Captain Murdoch remained on the wreck. There were two other boats on board, but, owing to the rapidity of the fire, they were early enveloped by flames. [Captain Murdoch] lowered himself into the water, and clung to a board he found floating. After being in the water for about twenty minutes, he was picked up by the yacht. In the meantime all was terror or despair on board the ill-fated vessel. While the greater part of the ship was a perfect volcano, the small quantity of gunpowder below exploded ... The cries of distress reached [those on board the yacht] at a considerable distance, and the poor wretches on the wreck swarmed like bees about the head of the vessel ...

At an early stage of the calamity the clothes of some of the females took fire, and the poor creatures ran madly amongst their unhappy comrades huddled together near the bow ... a young unmarried woman ... who was almost dead when brought on board the [rescuing ship] ... stated to us that long after the fire had broken out, somebody on deck – she thinks a female – tumbled her overboard, probably thinking that death by drowning would be a far preferable death for her than death by burning ... The young woman, however, after plunging into the water, was borne upon the tops of the waves. She seems to have floated... At length she caught hold of a hand. It was the hand of a dying woman. They seized each other with a sort of death-grasp, and for some time it was a kind of struggle with them as to who should be the conqueror or the last survivor of the two. The dying woman, however, who had been shattered about the head, from having been no doubt frequently driven against the hull of the burning vessel, breathed her last. Her head sank, but her body floated on the water. Our female informant held on by that dead body, and was absolutely saved by it.

This disaster occurred just a few miles away from the mouth of the Mersey, close to where the muddy river spilled into the sea at Liverpool. The *Ocean Monarch* had only recently left port, but luck alone meant assistance was available; there would have been no organised response from the mainland. Once a ship left the docks, or in some cases, after the tug towing a ship to deeper water had cast off its ropes, the captain, crew and any passengers travelling with them were effectively on their own.

There was also the weather to worry about. Sailing ships could drift for days if there was no breeze, or were easily blown off course by many miles during storms, their sails torn to useless rags. Most ships sprang leaks at some point on the long journey from England to Australia, while passing through different weathers and climates. The shrinking and swelling of the timbers sometimes led to gaps and draughts, or seawater leaking through. As one emigrant informed *Household Words* in 1853, by the time he arrived in Australian waters, 'The condition of our cabin – our berths – every cabin and every berth in the 'tween decks, no tongue can tell. All washed out, and everything left, not high and dry, but moist, rotten, broken, trodden up, strewn about, and turned to rags and slush'.

Rats and cockroaches often added to the emigrants' misery, and sometimes dogs were carried on board as ratters to keep the number of rodents down. One British traveller Mrs George Darby Griffith could put up with 'dirt and discomfort' but for the 'swarm of cockroaches that infest us; they almost drive me out of my senses'. She recalled in 1845 how: 'sixty were killed in our own cabin, and we might have killed as many more; they are very large, about two inches and a half long, and run about your pillows and sheets in a most disgusting manner'. In an attempt to protect herself from them as she lay in her bunk, she felt 'obliged to sleep with a great muslin veil over my face, which adds not a little to the heat and suffocation'. These were not the only night-time visitors to the long-suffering passengers. One man lay asleep on a table 'and was woken up by a huge monster running down one of the [ropes] into his shirt, and it was a long time before he could dispossess himself of his unwelcome visitor'.

Passengers might scrape together the money to buy the best class of ticket they could afford, in the hope of a healthier, more pleasant voyage. But, as one emigrant found to his horror, once on board ship passengers were entirely at the mercy of the captain and crew. Not only was he led to a dank and dingy area of steerage, the cheapest and most basic form of accommodation, instead of the second class berth he had paid for, he also had to do without any kind of sleeping quarters. Along with 50 or 60 others, he was left to improvise a berth with tables or a bare bit of floor, and once he saw how filthy the place was, he chose to sleep on the deck. This was probably the healthiest choice given the sanitary arrangements on board. *Reynolds's Newspaper* covered the swindled emigrant's case in revolting detail, revealing that there were 'but two water-closets for these sixty passengers, and as these were never cleaned, the soil from them ran upon the decks, and, mixing with the drippings of the pigsties and the scullery, rolled down upon the tables of the unfortunate passengers'.

If the passengers weren't poisoned by human waste dribbling onto their food and their faces in the night, then the meals served up to them were often enough to make them sick: '[T]he preserved meat, when the cases were opened, stunk aloud, the pork was quite green with putrefaction … and when complaint was made of hairs that were left on the meat, they were told that that was a delicacy. "It was a buffalo's hump." The biscuits were so ancient that the moment they were put on the table the weevils and maggots came out and began to walk off'. This sort of fare was unfortunately a regular occurrence at sea.

Both passengers (and crew) also faced considerable danger if they decided to take the air on deck during rough weather, as Barrow told the *Bradford Observer* in his account of travelling to Australia:

From the time of passing the Cape until the end of our journey, we had almost unceasing gales. We were frequently in peril; but only lost a few sails and light spars [thick wooden poles]. One night when the sea ran mountains high, and we were scudding before the gale under close-reefed topsails, a sailor fell from the rigging, overboard. One shriek and loud cry for help, and a tremendous wave carried him far away. Another sailor seized a life buoy, and was in the act of jumping over, when the captain grappled with him, and the two lay rolling and struggling on the deck together. No human power could have saved the poor fellow on such a night.

Seasickness made thousands of travellers miserable on their way to Australia. Preventative (and often completely useless) herbal tonics and pills were advertised, such as these tablets promoted in the *Stirling Observer* in 1853:

THE VEGETABLE RESTORATIVE PILLS, prepared by JOHN KAYE, Esq., are HARMLESS in their operation, being perfectly free from all manner of Poison: but they are at the same time powerful [enough] to conquer disease by thoroughly purifying the Blood … TO EMIGRANTS. Much inconvenience from Sea Sickness may be prevented by taking a few

doses prior to sailing, and in all our COLONIES they are very highly
esteemed. The Rev. W. Coggin, writing from Van Diemen's Land, says "All
who have tried them ... considered their introduction a perfect blessing."
Hundreds of Cases of Cure accompany each Box.

Just as they did on land, some passengers tried to drink their cares and
complaints away. 'On board ship there was drinking enough. People took
wine and brandy to keep away sea-sickness, or to cure them of it. But
I tasted nothing of the sort; and though sometimes a little squeamish, I
was never really sick, and never missed a meal', the Reverend W.B. Clarke
informed the *Dumfries and Galloway Standard* in 1853, regarding his
travels to Canada.

With water stored in tanks and barrels and gradually becoming so thick
with scum and tiny creatures that the liquid resembled a moving pea-soup
after a few months at sea, spirits might have been better for travellers'
health. Both on land and at sea people commonly drank weak beer rather
than water, but even so, some of those landing in Australia were shocked
at just how much alcohol was drunk there. 'It is alarming to think of
the quantity of drink that must be consumed here in the course of one
week. But it is very remarkable that very few really drunk people are to be
seen on the streets ... There are, however, to be seen now and again the
brandified snout and blotched visage crossing one's path while passing
along', one emigrant, John Youl, commented in the *Stirling Observer* in
1854.

There were plenty of threats to immigrants' health upon their arrival in
Australia, as John J.H. told readers of the *Dundee Courier* in 1853: 'As I
have fallen a victim to that dreaded malady dysentery, or bowel complaint,
and having got myself somewhat disfigured with the mosquitos, which are
flying about pretty thickly at this season, I have been unable to visit the
gold diggings ... It is, from all accounts, very dirty and dangerous work'.
Cholera, typhus, dysentery, and venereal disease all followed the travellers
across the ocean.

Blowflies, yet another hazard, buzzed round the settlers and caused great
disgust. One settler, William Howlitt, wrote in 1855:

The other day Charlton was skinning a flying squirrel just shot, and it was crawling with live maggots before he had finished. The other day we saw an ox in a dray, which had its eye burst, and there were actually dozens of maggots in it, eating it out. But stranger still, a gentleman in a party working near us, hurt his eye with the handle of a windlass; and the next morning feeling a strange creeping sensation in it, he got up and to his horror actually saw it alive with maggots.

As Howlitt was to discover, blowflies do not lay eggs on food sources, but wriggling maggots. He went on to describe flies, ants, centipedes, scorpions and spiders as being 'a terrific nuisance', and their bites as 'severe and venomous'.

In this dangerous and initially inhospitable climate there was great demand for surgeons and many adventurous young doctors travelled out to Australia, among them a young Scot, Robert Hannay Cunningham. Cunningham worked his passage out as a ship surgeon in July 1852. On his arrival in Melbourne the 27-year-old doctor set up shop in one of the 'Tent Cities' then springing up as the pre-Gold Rush lodging houses and shacks filled to overflowing. It would have been a world away from his home in Glasgow, but with parrots and cockatiels flying through the shady green trees and a constant flow of patients, his new life was still an interesting one and full of promise. So good, in fact, that around the time Captain Noble was supervising construction of the iron clipper *Tayleur*, and the pardoned convict Samuel Carby sailed to England as a free man, the doctor decided to return to Scotland to collect his family. This would prove to be a terrible mistake.

Chapter Two

On landing [in Melbourne] I found even the small quantity of luggage I had with me very cumbersome ... I would advise you not to trouble yourselves with any luggage further than what will hold your outfit for the voyage, as storage room is ... very difficult to be got. I would advise you also not to bring any bank orders with you, or you will certainly rue it ... [T]here is nothing like the hard cash, whether in sovereigns or in silver.

After wearying my already tired legs in searching for a domicile I was forced to take up my abode in a place that looked more like a pig stye than a human dwelling place ... It is a house partly built of wood, with day light shining through the roof, and as for the door, the wind blows it open, even when it is locked ... it is only individuals who know somewhat of agricultural pursuits, or who can brave out a severe storm of wind and rain, that are needed here, and not those genteel and fanciful folks who would faint and die under one of those hurricanes with which we are occasionally visited.

We had one of those storms on Sabbath last. The wind blew from the north, exceedingly hot, the dust flying in the air almost as thick as ever you saw the smoke ascending from one of the tall chimneys in Glasgow, accompanied with the most terrific peals of thunder and vivid flashes of lightning, followed by long-continued torrents of rain.

(Letter from John J.H. published in the *Dundee Courier*, 20 April 1853)

Tuesday 4 October 1853,
Warrington Bank Quay Foundry, Cheshire

The day of the *Tayleur*'s launch dawned with a low grey ceiling of cloud reaching across the rooftops of Warrington to the hills of nearby Runcorn. Cool breezes ruffled the bunting draped near the stern of the *Tayleur*, slapping it against the sides of the wooden platforms rigged up for the dignitaries due to arrive later. Six months of hard work were about to reach an exhilarating end for those who had sweated over the largest merchant sailing ship in the world. This event would mark the beginning of an exciting new era of development and trade for this old inland town.

With the launch of RMS *Tayleur* Warrington would become known throughout the world as a town capable of building the most technologically advanced ships. Twenty miles of shallow riverbed and dogleg turns had previously caused Warrington to be overlooked when companies sought a yard to build an ocean-going vessel. Yet the makers of the *Tayleur*, the Bank Quay Foundry, had faith in the tide and the pilots employed to guide ships past the sandbanks and submerged rocks between Warrington and the Port of Liverpool. Today the tide was low but creeping higher along the banks of the Mersey; the lines of miniature buoys laid out to guide the iron clipper towards the Liverpool docks bobbed in the water, waiting for the tugboats and massive ship to race past on the highest tide.

Men rushed about in the foundry yard, and factory workers and shop staff hastened to finish their tasks as the townsfolk had been granted a rare half-day holiday to celebrate the launch. However, the captain of the new ship was nowhere to be seen. Twenty-nine-year-old John Noble, a nautical hero of the Gold Rush era, had been injured after falling from the forecastle into the main hold of the ship just a few hours before. He plummeted 25 feet onto a deck crowded with spars and tools – the height of a two-storey house. Severely shaken, but with no other injuries apparent, Captain Noble had to leave the launch to others. It was an ill omen.

The great and the good of Warrington arriving by carriage, cart and train included the mayor, several MPs, the eminent local historian William Beamont, and a handful of clergymen. A bottle of christening wine festooned with red ribbons had been set aside for the daughter of North Lancashire MP J. Wilson Patten to smash on the *Tayleur*'s painted metal hull. Meanwhile the kitchen staff of the Patten Arms hotel were preparing refreshments for the party at the works.

But there was another absence that day, one more keenly felt among the crowd of dignitaries than that of the unlucky captain. Charles Tayleur, founder of the Vulcan Foundry and Engineering Works, the company that had built the great ship now waiting in the dock, was represented only by the figurehead carved in his image. Its eyes stared sightless from the prow of the enormous ship above white-whiskered cheeks and a dark frock coat, while the real Charles Tayleur mourned the recent loss of his wife Jane.

A local journalist walked among the townsfolk, observing the mingling of the classes during the festivities for the *Warrington Guardian*. His eye was caught by a councillor 'with that expression of senatorial gravity which a year of office never fails to give … heightened more by the importance of the occasion' amid the merchants, tradesmen, labourers and mechanics thronging the riverbank for a look at the *Tayleur*. Their wives and daughters came too, hundreds of them on foot, others in horse-drawn carriages, horses' hooves clattering on the cobbles while the 'Lancashire witches', as the journalist dubbed them, screamed 'pretty cries of delight' and stood 'with gloved hands clasped in earnest admiration'.

Soon after 1 pm the water rose even higher than hoped for, and the sturdy workmen's arms rose and fell as they hammered out the wedges of wood holding the ship in place on the dock. The vessel moved slowly at first, inch by inch, as the men sang together over the din of their hammers beating in unison. On the riverbanks men held women and children aloft for a clearer view, ignoring the cold water soaking their feet and clothing. Skirts rising up in the river around the women and girls revealed scandalous expanses of flesh; bloomers were still a luxury among the lower classes. Old men grew nimble for the day, clambering up ladders and across poles, balancing precariously on timbers as they hung on to masonry to keep themselves steady. Boats upstream held hundreds vying for a glimpse of the ship, and there was a general atmosphere of excitement and the expectation that this would lead to a more prosperous future.

At 1.25 pm someone shouted that the ship was off; at that moment Miss Patten swung the bottle against the stern:

> *the baptismal wine scattered to the winds, and … to a deafening shout from the assembled thousands … the* Tayleur *floated swiftly and gracefully into the Mersey. So beautifully clean was the launch, that it seemed to take all by surprise, and it was a second or two before admiration merged into gratitude, and a second shout louder than the first greeted her as she drew up by the bank-side, and slowly turned to the spectators her whole length, as three steamers took her in tow for Liverpool.*

The filthy river water rose as the mighty ship carved its way through the Mersey, soaking bystanders watching from the banks. The local journalist wrote a tongue-in-cheek description of 'men guiltless of a bath before, now undergoing the "water cure" of their temerity … It was a most amusing thing to see delicate ladies, and brawny men, and even policemen, who were there to keep the ground, not being able to keep their own, but with hands aloft, and boots be-bogged, at last running from a danger they had never *apprehended'*.

Speeches were made on behalf of the owners and by the manager of the Bank Quay Foundry from the steamers in the water and the bunting-clad platforms. The crowd cheered them as the sky dimmed and the rain fell. The party of local worthies dispersed, some taking a tour of the interior of the foundry, toasting the health of the workers and enjoying the food laid on by the Patten Arms. Others, including the mayor, swiftly climbed into the little boats waiting to accompany the *Tayleur* as she was guided towards the nearby town of Runcorn for the night.

A Captain Foulkes temporarily replaced the shaken Captain Noble at the helm of the *Tayleur* for the first leg of her journey. Foulkes was Superintendent of Lights and Buoys to the Duke of Bridgewater's Navigation, with plenty of experience in sailing the Mersey; an excellent choice to pilot the *Tayleur* through the channel. He was assisted by three small tugs, the *Victory*, *Gleaner* and *Reaper*, all accustomed to towing vessels from port to port along the river, and the guideposts and miniature buoys he had spent months placing carefully in the water. They marked the safest channel for the mighty ship, which at approximately 2,000 tons was about 40 times the size of the usual barges known as Mersey flats. These barges ferried goods from quay to canal and many ports in-between and their sails, the colour of brick-dust, were a common sight in the Warrington waterways.

Townspeople clustered along the eight-mile route, braving the increasingly foul weather to watch the spectacle, including one young boy, John Corbett, from the Quaker School in Penketh. John would write of the excitement many decades later. He sat with his teacher and classmates near a tight bend in the river, where the Mersey meets the Sankey canal. The schoolchildren had a lucky escape when the *Tayleur* broke free of the cables tethering her to the boats towing her downstream. The sides of the ship towered above them, the figurehead looming large over the sharp bows as the *Tayleur* swung close to the bank and straight at the children sitting there. She pushed the starboard tug right out of the water and up the muddy bank, almost ramming the lock wall where the schoolchildren sat, before the port-side tug went astern on full power, engine revving and sending up smoke. The *Tayleur* cleared the bend with just a few feet to spare, leaving shocked spectators and the grounded tug behind her.

The tide was running quickly down the Mersey. The weather had worsened and the situation looked grim, but luckily hundreds of navvies were working nearby, building the Manchester-Garston railway. Pausing to watch the ship drift past, the labourers heard the shouts of those on board. An engineer called out a plan to the rest of the men, who immediately sprinted to nearby piles of slender scaffold poles and ran with them to the little steamboat. Dozens of poles were thrust against the side of the tug, 20 men to a pole, as if they had been trained for just such an emergency. At the word of command, the men pushed the vessel down the muddy slope and into the river, wading deep into the water to make sure the tug was in far enough. Soaked to the skin, the rest of the day's hard labour still ahead of them, the navvies watched as the vessel got back up to speed and raced to overtake the *Tayleur* and resume her duty.

The Mersey runs west from Stockport for 68 miles, passing through Warrington and Runcorn before surging into the Irish Sea via Liverpool Bay. This stretch of the river, usually crowded with an odorous mixture of loaded boats, and industrial as well as human waste, remained clear of traffic to allow the iron clipper and her escort to sail unhindered downstream. Small vessels soon followed, packed with sightseers unafraid of the wet weather. Approaching Moore, a low-lying Cheshire village with views of the Welsh mountains, the *Tayleur* appeared to be cruising through fields and forest, tall and silent, save for the puttering engines of the tugs and applause of onlookers.

The ship wound her way cautiously through the curving channel, as the ebb tide quickened and pulled her from the marshes towards the towns of Runcorn and Widnes. Sodden spectators crowded the hill topped by the low brown ruins of Halton Castle to watch her progress. Once a health resort, Runcorn was now, like Warrington, a hub of soap manufacturing and tanning, turning the river into a stinking murk of effluent and industrial overflow. The Mersey narrows here to just a quarter of a mile across, and only a few weeks prior to this the *Anne Chesshyre* had been launched from a shipyard next to the Old Quay. Crafted from thick planks of wood from Britain's dwindling forests, the *Anne Chesshyre* was the largest ship Runcorn had ever produced. The *Tayleur* had four times her displacement, moving quadruple the water the *Anne Chesshyre* had below her hull. Riding high on the water, the tide buoying the iron clipper, the *Tayleur*'s three masts rose as tall as the steeple of the new pink sandstone church spiking Runcorn's skyline.

Sand accumulates in the bends of rivers, and Runcorn Gap was no different. Even with the tide helping her on her way, there was a lot of concern about whether the *Tayleur* would make it downriver or come to rest on the sandbanks. The idea of fitting her with enormous wheels for the purpose of getting over them had been given serious thought, but she made it past the Church Bank and the long bar of Hurst Rocks to the deepest part of the channel. Anchored there fore and aft, secure despite the movement of the tide, she was watched over by the men on the little boat *Plutas*. They were monitoring the situation for the Bridgewater Trustees, a small group in charge of the local water traffic. The crowds observed from the riverbanks as she was made fast and loaded with 100 tons of coal at each end. This ballasted her in the water and prevented her from heeling over with the wind or the movement of the tide.

With the *Tayleur* safely moored until morning, the river men took to the water once again, the Mersey's surface cluttered with small sightseers' vessels, shrimping boats, ferries, barges and Mersey flats. The dignitaries and sailors aboard the *Gleaner*, *Victory* and *Reaper* bid farewell and started the return leg of their journey back to Bank Quay in Warrington. As the tide receded, birds flocked to the mud to pick at the debris left behind. Gulls screamed as they paddled with pale feet and stretched their wings menacingly at competitors vying for the scraps. The traffic withdrew to the safe moorings on either side of the river and, aside from the men of the *Plutas*, the skeleton crew aboard the *Tayleur* were alone on the Mersey.

Back in Warrington, as John Corbett later recalled, he and his friends were having fun at school in Penketh. It was dark outside, a cold and wet autumnal afternoon, and the place was abuzz with talk of the *Tayleur* and their narrow escape. One lad, Jim Thompson, sat drawing at his desk. When the other children saw the subject of his sketch, they ripped it to shreds in fury. The press had made much of the *Tayleur*'s strength, safety and modern design. She was top-of-the-line and *the* ship to take a berth on if you happened to be travelling to the Australian Gold Rush. So why had young Jim pictured her wrecked beneath steep cliffs, waves breaking over her slanting decks?

Chapter Three

This is with us the beginning of spring. The gardens are full of peach and fig trees, grape vines, &c., all budding and blossoming ready for Christmas. Then, when you are seated by a blazing fire, consuming your plum puddings, and listening to the pattering hail or drifting snow outside, we shall be eating ours beneath a blazing sun, with an attendant cloud of tropical mosquitoes. Then the trees will be burnt brown, and the pastures be dried up. At present all is green and refreshful; the hedges displaying huge cactuses, and the fields bringing forth spontaneously, many of the expensively pampered varieties of English greenhouses. Still, with all the wild luxuriances of Australian vegetation, and admitting its oftentimes bold and striking landscapes, it does not, so far as I have yet seen, bear comparison with the scenery of our own dear England. But I forget that I am as yet but a stranger here; perhaps when I have seen more I may speak differently.

(J.H. Barrow, the *Bradford Observer*, 5 January 1854)

Saturday 14 to Thursday 19 January 1854, Liverpool

RMS *Tayleur* was initially advertised as departing the port of Liverpool on 20 November 1853. However, problems with sourcing parts and fitting out the luxurious A1-class ship meant that this was put back several times, until the White Star Line published a final departure date: noon on Thursday 19 January 1854. The White Star Line were keen to publicise their 'truly splendid vessel' and provided plenty of copy for the press, boasting that 'the largest merchantman ever built in England will undoubtedly prove to be the fastest of the Australian fleet'. Many newspapers commented on her vast size, the ample accommodation for passengers and their belongings, and the amount of ventilation and light available below deck. The press heralded the *Tayleur* as 'superior to any ship hitherto dispatched to the Australian colonies'.

But the *Tayleur*'s captain, John Noble, was the main draw for passengers. Travelling halfway round the world required a great deal of nerve, trust in a captain and his ship, and sometimes desperation. A captain's good name – or otherwise – helped many a passenger select the vessel that would be their home during a dangerous few months on the ocean. The Chief Examiner of Masters and Mates in Liverpool had been asked by the *Tayleur*'s owners to recommend an able and experienced captain for the Liverpool-Australia route; someone suited to the new age of iron clippers. He immediately proposed Captain Noble, describing him as 'the most eligible man who could be selected to command the post'. This was a significant step up the career ladder for Noble. He gave up his command of the wooden clipper *Australia* for the chance to captain what was considered to be one of the fastest ships afloat. Noble had just spent 13 months at sea with the *Australia*, on what was hailed by the *Liverpool Courier* as 'one of the most memorable voyages on record'. He had taken emigrants – including the brother of one passenger on the *Tayleur* – to Melbourne, then sailed on to China, the West Indies and finally home to the crowded port of Liverpool.

Visitors to the mighty ship were amazed by the amount of space and luxury on board. One reporter wrote in the *Liverpool Courier* of the *Tayleur*'s permanent staircases, which allowed passengers and crew ease of access between the upper and passenger decks and would have been far safer in a rough sea than the usual ladders propped under hatches in the top deck, especially for women in ankle-length dresses. He also enthused over the *Tayleur*'s size and safety, stating that 'the largest iron sailing vessel afloat [is] a particularly strong ship … no expense or skill has been spared to render her perfect as an iron ship of the very strongest construction'.

Death and disease accompanied every ship passing the equator, with mortality statistics for incoming vessels a regular feature in the Australian press and burials at sea accepted as an inevitable hazard by passengers and crew. Just two years before, the *Lady Montague* sailed for California via Van Diemen's Land and lost 293 of the 500 souls aboard to disease and suicide. Much was made of the *Tayleur*'s arrangements for carrying fresh air below deck, with reports of sidelights opening in every room, as well as skylights and ventilators allowing light and sea breezes to freshen the passengers' quarters even in the roughest of weather.

Some mid-nineteenth century emigrant ships were little better than the early transportation vessels used to relocate convicts in the late 1700s, some of which arrived in port with only half their original consignment still alive. Both government-funded and private travel were still very loosely regulated in the mid-1800s. Parliament commissioned a report into the conditions for emigrants below decks, which included this account of steerage travel by Lieutenant Charles Friend RN, just ten years before the *Tayleur* took on her passengers:

It was scarcely possible to induce the passengers to sweep the decks after their meals or to be decent in their common wants of nature; in many cases in bad weather, they would not go on deck, their health suffered so much that their strength was gone, and they had not the power to help themselves. Hence the between decks were like a loathsome dungeon. When hatchways were opened, under which the people were stowed, the steam arose and the stench was like that from a pen of pigs. The few beds they had were in a dreadful state, for the straw once wet with seawater, soon rotted, besides which they used the between decks for every filthy purpose.

Whenever vessels put back from distress all these miseries and suffering were exhibited in the most aggravated form. In one case it appeared that the vessel having experienced rough weather, the people were unable to go on deck and cook their provisions: the strongest maintained the upper hand over the weakest and it was said that there were women who died of starvation. At that time the passengers were expected to cook for themselves and from their being unable to do so the greatest suffering arose. It was naturally at the commencement of the voyage that this system produced the worst effects. For the first days were those in which the people suffered most from sea sickness and under the prostration of body thereby induced, were wholly incapacitated from cooking. Thus though provisions might be abundant the passengers would be half starved.

The medical inspection required by law before any passengers left port consisted of little more than a glance from a government agent. Still, one woman and her young son were excluded from the *Tayleur* as the little boy had chickenpox, and they were forced to return to port. This must have been upsetting but they would soon realise what a lucky escape they had had.

Passenger ships were also obliged to have a surgeon aboard. Dr Robert Hannay Cunningham, a native of Pittarthie, Fife, was an experienced Surgeon Superintendent having worked his passage from England to Australia 18 months earlier on the *Mirzapore*. He had studied medicine in Edinburgh and married Susan Wyse, the daughter of a fellow surgeon, in 1848, their first child, Henry, arriving 10 months later. Dr Cunningham was no stranger to fresh starts in new places. He had travelled to Peru before practising medicine in the well-to-do area of West Regent Street, Glasgow. As the second son of a wealthy clansman, he had little hope of inheriting the family home of Kingsmuir and sought to build a new life for his growing family in Melbourne instead.

Dr Cunningham specialised in 'midwifery and the diseases of women and children', according to his adverts, but he also gave vaccinations and treated the poor for free. In Australia's canvas cities, where hundreds of tents covered muddy ground and there was little organisation, security or privacy, Dr Cunningham's tent could be 'distinguished by a golden ball atop a square blue flag'. He prospered in Melbourne, moving from a tent to an apartment in the space of just a few months, and became convinced that this was the best place to raise his family.

Cunningham arrived back in Scotland around the time the *Tayleur* was being launched into the Mersey. By now Henry was four, and had a one-year-old brother, George, who would be meeting his father for the first time. Dr Cunningham wasted no time in ordering a portable shop and attached four-bedroom house to be shipped from Leith to Melbourne. Made from metal to his precise instructions, the structure would serve as surgery, apothecary and home for the family of four and their servant.

A bright, personable young man, Cunningham was working his passage aboard the *Tayleur* for the nominal wage of a shilling. His youngest son George was one of 14 infants on board, while his wife and Elizabeth Shepphard, his children's nurse, were two of approximately 100 women immigrating to the chaotic shores of Melbourne.

Those sailing to the goldfields of Australia were mainly men who were affluent enough to make arrangements for the voyage and travel to Liverpool but not sufficiently wealthy to lead comfortable lives in their country of origin. People who had a little money, sufficient for food and a dry place to sleep at night, were feeling the pressure from the influx of cheap labour from Ireland, and the resulting lack of housing and jobs. Despite financial aid from the church, other countries and individual philanthropists, Ireland was still in a bad way after the potato blight of the 1840s. Those who had survived were weak, poor and often lacking land and seed potatoes to plant in it, so many Irish people fled 'from famine and pestilence' in search of better lives.

There were at least 111 Irish passengers aboard the *Tayleur*, joining 78 Scots, hundreds of English and Welsh, and travellers from Europe and America, as well as crewmen from Italy, India, and China. The majority of passengers had raised enough money to pay for the voyage to Australia; some, including the Hendersons of Aberdeen, were assisted by charitable organisations, such as the Religious Society of Friends. Others appear to have acquired the cash for their fares using less honest means.

Many of the emigrants travelling to the Gold Rush intended to send for their families later, while others changed their names on the voyage or on entering Australia and started afresh. Personal history was largely irrelevant in a place where health, fitness and an appetite for hard work were essential, and criminal records were common. An anonymous visitor to the *Tayleur* noted of the passengers: 'The great majority belonged to the farming, mining, or artisan classes with only a very small number rating as clerks and they were mostly robust youths fit for any sort of work. There were some families numbering from four to five to six but few were of tender years'.

Of the 650 people officially aboard the *Tayleur*, 14 babies and 56 children appear on the various lists. Many of the families would never have seen the sea before, let alone travelled on board a ship. They may have sought guidance from pamphlets and guidebooks available for a couple of pence, such as *The Emigrants' Voyages Manual*, which suggested singing as a pastime: 'Thus are the angels employed. But let me urge you not to sing frivolous or indecent songs. If your companions commence any ribaldry stop them at once. Remember, on that very night a fearful storm may arise and you may be called into the presence of your maker'.

This would have seemed quite possible to those on board the *Tayleur*, especially on a cold grey January day with the papers full of news of shipwrecks such as the *Lady Evelyn* recently lost off Taiwan (then Formosa) on her way to San Francisco. Of 250 aboard, only 30 survived. The number of ships known to have wrecked in British waters in 1852 totalled a staggering 1,115 vessels. Yet the *Tayleur* was so big, new and fastidiously appointed that the idea of any wave mastering her could easily be dismissed as fanciful – in port, at least.

Potential emigrants had a difficult choice to make when arranging their journey. They could travel in the winter when cholera, a scourge of Victorian Britain, was inactive but the weather was rough, or set off in the summer, when it was milder and the waves were calmer, but the ships were also busy and rife with disease. The *Tayleur*, with her modern design and celebrated captain, seemed like a safe bet. Some of the passengers had already travelled from France or Germany and many from famine-ravaged Ireland on leaky old boats. When they boarded the brand new *Tayleur*, optimism was in the cold moist January air.

It was customary for passenger ships to have a Christian service performed on board prior to departure. On an inclement Sunday morning a couple of days before the *Tayleur* set off, Reverend James Buck of the Liverpool Seamen's Friend Society travelled up the river in a little boat to hold one. He found Captain Noble and his new wife, Anne, on board and they quickly made their way to the passenger deck, as it was far too wet and windy to hold the service out in the open.

Reverend Buck clambered onto a small box and took off his hat. Over 200 passengers crowded round and stood in silence for a moment of quiet blessing. As the rain lashed the sides of the ship, drumming the deck above their heads, all eyes were on the preacher, the floor rocking gently beneath their feet. Satisfied, he gestured to them and they sang hymns, voices together as one. Then they 'prayed for the divine blessing on the ship, the crew, and their officers and commander, and all the passengers whose temporary house she was to be for so long a voyage, not forgetting those who were left behind at home, or those who had preceded them in their departure from the land of their birth, and were now upon the great sea'. Their song filled the space below deck in glorious harmony once again, drowning out the rain and the slap of small waves against the hull, then all was silent.

The Reverend stepped down from the box and accepted their thanks. Those passengers and crew present were reportedly delighted to receive the Bibles and religious tracts he had arranged to have delivered, and parcels of leaflets were left in the empty bunks of those still to join the ship. Written especially by the Religious Tract Society for those heading for the heat of the Gold Rush, the tracts included vigorous statements like: 'The exodus still continues. With what eager rapidity one multitude follows another. The great army moves on, its footsteps lead to the sea, its heart meditating battle with the wilderness and the scrub and the uncultivated virgin soil and thirsting for the golden spoil of lands which their fathers knew not'.

Congratulating the Reverend Buck warmly on his sermon, the passengers filled his portfolio with the names and addresses of loved ones they had left behind. The Reverend promised to send their families printed accounts of his service and visit to the luxury ship. Buck later wrote: 'Many afterwards testified that it was a very solemn season, when fathers, mothers, and young people of both sexes, came to say farewell'. For some of the passengers it would be the last service they would hear in England. But they soon cast the serious mood aside.

Their spirits buoyed by Buck's words of positivity and hope, they gathered in the saloon for light refreshments. The worst of the goodbyes and drudgery of hauling luggage and goods was now over and the time for casting off rapidly approaching. The Reverend said his farewells then transferred from the iron clipper to a small steamer, which chugged him along the grey waters of the Mersey estuary to another emigrant ship, the *Indian Queen*. Chartered by Pilkington and Wilson, the same company leasing the somewhat larger *Tayleur*, the *Indian Queen* was a wooden clipper also scheduled to depart for Melbourne that Thursday at noon. It was a race between old and new, traditional design versus modern technology, as the *Liverpool Mercury* quipped: 'the ships are competing and an interesting race is anticipated'.

Although most passengers were now aboard and settling into their allotted spaces – sleeping in their three-tiered trough bunks and getting used to the gentle motion of the river before they took to the sea – both passengers and crew still had a lot to do in the three days leading up to their departure. Captain Noble had engaged the last of the crew just a few days prior. Many of them came from the sailors' home intended to keep them safe from prostitutes and rogues while ashore. Noble later revealed that 'the whole of the crew, with the exception of the mate, were strangers' to him. There would be a lot of attention on the crew later, and their mixture of abilities, experience and nationality, but there was nothing unusual in the complement, although the low numbers were a problem.

There were strict rules regarding crews and the tonnage of ships, especially for vessels chartered by the government, but the *Tayleur* was not part of any government enterprise. Also, since the way the tonnage of ships was measured had changed in some ports but not others – including Liverpool – the *Tayleur* had the number of crewmen required by law, but only because she was measured in this particular port. Under the old system, the *Tayleur* measured as 1,640 tons and three men for every 100 tons had been legally required as sufficient to keep the ship functioning. But the new system meant the *Tayleur* came in at a significantly heavier 1,979 tons, so an additional nine men should have been aboard and working the ship. Another issue, which was not considered when the tonnage system was discussed, was the fact that iron ships gave their crews a lot more to do.

Ships made of wood had thick walls and required enormous frames to keep their hulls from collapsing under the weight of the cargo and the pressure of heavy seas. Iron ships, however, had much thinner walls. The local paper claimed the *Tayleur* was able to hold almost double the tonnage of a similarly sized wooden ship, which made her extremely profitable for her owners, although also more difficult for the crew to handle. The crew had nearly twice as many boxes, barrels and parcels to secure throughout the storms and fluctuating temperatures, which would make the ropes holding them fast alternately loosen and shrink. There was more space for the passengers, but this also gave the crew more to take care of.

Many of the sailors who signed up for the voyage to Melbourne were working their passage for a nominal shilling, like Dr Cunningham, and planned to leave the harbour for the goldfields on arrival. Some were experienced seamen while others, in the words of one passenger, 'were only lads' and out of six apprentices, four were completely new to the sea. From a crew of 71, 16 were on board to take care of the passengers as stewards and cooks, and 55 to handle the ship. Charles Griffiths, aged 29, was working his passage to Melbourne. Together with his wife Sarah and their ten-month-old son, Arthur, the family were embarking on a life-changing voyage. Charles had worked for a clergyman in the tiny village of Barbadoes, Monmouthshire, before moving north to Hereford, where Sarah had kept a small cookshop at the bottom of Eign Street, half a mile from the cathedral. Cookshops were usually run in the front room of a house and rarely very profitable, but it would have allowed her to care for their baby while she worked.

On board ship Sarah would have to get used to other people cooking for her family, which may even have been a relief with a ten-month-old child to look after. The passengers in each class of accommodation were catered for by cooking staff employed by the captain. These galley staff prepared meals specified in a menu set out by an Act of Parliament, using rations doled out daily by the stewards, sometimes supplemented by provisions the passengers brought with them. As a traveller recommended in the *Dundee, Perth and Cupar Advertiser* in 1853, those who 'wish to enjoy a few home comforts on the ocean' should take 'a few pots of preserves, a few of pickles, which are a great treat, a little good cheese, a few fresh-laid eggs preserved in salt, a dried musked ham or two (home cured do not keep in the tropics), and a few dried Portugal or English onions, or any other little luxury they may prefer'.

He also recommended that they bring bottles of ground coffee and some tea as 'the latter is generally a common or damaged article on shipboard, and the coffee is served out green, and there is consequently much trouble in getting it roasted and ground'. As for alcohol, 'All who would like a little ale or porter would do well to bring a small cask or two, as the tropical heat invariably breaks bottles. These things on shipboard are certainly considered luxuries, yet a pound or two spent in their purchases will undoubtedly prove beneficial to health, as well as afford an agreeable change in diet'.

All but first class passengers received basic rations consisting mainly of suet, beef, bread, oatmeal, raisins, potatoes, pickles and peas. They could drink water, tea or coffee, as well as the lime juice prescribed to help passengers and crew avoid the dreaded scurvy resulting from a diet lacking in Vitamin C. Richard Hawkins, an English sailor in the late 1500s, described 'the scars of wounds which had for many years been healed, [being] forced open again by this virulent distemper', 'denting of the flesh of the legs with a mans finger, the pit remayning without filling up in a good space', and 'putrid gums' becoming so soft and jellied that teeth would fan out at right angles under the slightest pressure. Children aged from one to 12 were given half rations.

Menus were often advertised in the press to reassure potential passengers and crew about the quality and variety of food they could expect to consume throughout the several months aboard a particular vessel. With no refrigeration and poor understanding of the science behind the spoiling of food and water, keeping supplies fresh and edible was a problem. Salted pork and dried peas were staples of the seafarers' diet. In 1761, a civil servant called William Thompson wrote of ship's bread being 'so full of large black-headed maggots that the men have [become] so nauseated [at] the thoughts of it as to be obliged to shut their eyes to confine that sense from being offended before they could bring their minds into the resolution of consuming it … [T]he beer … stunk as abominably as the foul stagnant water which is pumped out of many cellars in London at midnight hour'. Thankfully for the *Tayleur* passengers, the general standard of supplies had since improved.

Those in second class accommodation received a larger quantity of rations than steerage and intermediate passengers, and also had their meals supplemented with half a pound of cheese per week. First class passengers had cutlery and tableware provided for them and dined at the captain's table, rather than with the rest of the passengers at one of the long wooden benches between the cheaper sleeping areas. They paid between £45 and £60 for the privilege – second class tickets were about £25, and steerage around £15 – and this premium fare included bedding, a two-berth cabin, a steward dedicated to their comfort and plenty of room for luggage. It also meant that they could look forward to devouring 'livestock in liberal quantity provided throughout the voyage' and being 'waited on as if in a hotel'.

The *Liverpool Mercury* later reported that the cooking galley in the *Tayleur* 'was well provided with efficient cooks and had been proved while the ship was in the river to be capable of fully performing all that could be required of it'. Their reporter was also impressed with the 'clear and ample space along her entire length for the operations of the crew. These were mustered ... on the quarter deck on Wednesday afternoon, and afforded as fair a specimen of their class as could be desired. The officers appeared to be most active and intelligent men'.

Fourteen of the seamen on board the *Tayleur* were from overseas, and all but three could speak or understand spoken English. Some had sailed together before, but for most of the diverse group this was the first time they had met. Nevertheless, the men worked tirelessly at the beginning of the week to ready the ship for her long voyage south of the equator. They loaded the passengers' luggage and cargo, cleared the deck, and hung small boats from high metal frames called davits to keep them out of the way of those on deck. The vessels had previously been used for chasing and harpooning whales and were often bought for merchant ships on the cheap. They could be used as lifeboats, for taking on supplies, exchanging news between passing ships or for retrieving items lost overboard, but there was only room for a few dozen in them – certainly not the roughly 650 people aboard.

A new tank of fresh water for drinking, cooking and washing acted as ballast in the hold, its cleanliness another advantage for the *Tayleur* passengers and crew. Thirteen years before, an expert witness, Dr John Wilson, gave testimony on the state of ship drinking-water in a Parliamentary Report, describing 'drinking water so putrid and offensive, often so thick and green from vegetable decomposition, and emitting so strongly the foetor of rotten eggs, as to disgust at once the sense of smell and of taste'.

The *Tayleur*'s water tank lay deep in the hold, along with plentiful goods mainly intended for sale and including everything a growing colony might desire. As yet there was no organized manufacturing in Australia. Farmers, labourers and all kinds of craftsmen had deserted their jobs in the hope of striking it rich on the goldfields. Many basic goods had to be imported from home, so the *Tayleur* was loaded with bricks and roofing slates, galvanised and bar iron, sheet lead, anvils, wood, and six tons of zinc. Most of the people out hunting for gold had nothing but canvas to call home in the crowded 'Tent Cities'. It wasn't just gold diggers who were making their fortunes in Australia; those working to support them were also turning a profit.

Fifteen tons of wire fencing, seven ploughs, three cast-iron cranes, a cask of rivets, fireplaces, three bundles of cart covers, bales of cloth and leather, hogsheads of blue and white chinaware, four cases of flint glass, a box of lamps and lanterns, boxes of tinplate, bottled beer and Sicilian wine, hats and harnesses, a vast amount of sawn timber, saddles, 30 blank gravestones and a piano were carefully packed into the hold, then finally a little wooden steamboat meant for the Australian rivers was loaded onto the deck. The *Tayleur*'s crew fastened the vessel securely into place, ready for its engineer and his wife to take up residence in its minuscule cabin throughout the voyage to Melbourne.

There were also the stores of food; enough for 650 people to have three meals per day. Any fresh food the passengers and crew brought aboard would have soon run out, and the cooks employed by the White Star Line to cater for the passengers did their best with the strict menus, despite the slight roll of the ship. It would be nothing compared to the movement of the Irish Sea in a few days' time.

The *Tayleur* now sat a foot and a half deeper in the water, but continued to tower over the warehouses and ships surrounding it. At four times the size of the average Liverpudlian ship, she drew attention even in a town with 'an immense multitude of vessels ensconced in the docks where the masts make an intricate forest for miles up and down the Liverpool shore', as Nathaniel Hawthorne described it. The writer of *The Scarlet Letter* was living in Liverpool at the time of the *Tayleur*'s launch. Employed as the United States consul, the best-paid position in the US Foreign Office, Hawthorne was not enamoured of the Mersey, describing it as 'the colour of a mud-puddle; and no atmospheric effect, so far as I have seen, ever gives it a more agreeable tinge'.

The poor weather may have made the river look unappealing, but the water was smooth enough to allow the final inspections on the *Tayleur* to continue. Lieutenant Prior, an Emigration Commissioner for the busy port of Liverpool, had the task of checking whether the *Tayleur* crew was sufficient and appropriate. He agreed the vessel was in good order and the crew were suitable for their roles on board ship, and turned a blind eye to the mess of items littering the upper deck. But according to John Aislabie, an upholsterer from Hull sailing in the second class section with his wife and four-year-old-daughter, 'The riggers were at work to the last moment before we sailed, and even worked on Sunday … We had riggers on board up to the moment of starting'.

* * *

Samuel Carby, a passenger in the intermediate section, would probably have been somewhat oblivious to the preparations as he was getting reacquainted with his own recently-wedded spouse below deck. Samuel and Sarah had been on the point of marriage when, in 1841, Samuel was sentenced to ten years' transportation for 'sheep-slaughtering'. According to reports in the papers, Sarah had 'loved not wisely but too well', and Samuel was a rogue deserving punishment.

Sarah had been in court during his trial, and was, according to a melodramatic report in the *Lincolnshire Chronicle*, 'indulging in the anxious hope that the jury would acquit him'. The newspaper continued, 'The delivery of the sentence was the precursor of a painful scene. Sarah shrieked, threw her arm around the prisoner's neck, and became overpowered with grief'. After he was sent out of the country she supported herself and their son Robert by making stays (a type of corset). Sarah lived with her parents and elder brother in Stamford, and Robert was raised as her brother and given the surname Bunning. The space for his father's name was also left blank on his birth certificate, despite Samuel's public acknowledgement of paternity before he left the country. Transportation was a death sentence of sorts, with many convicts dying on the way to the Antipodes; suffering illness, violence, or hanged for further crimes while out there.

Twelve years passed without Sarah hearing a word from Samuel. Then one October morning, as she took the train from Morcott to Stamford, Sarah found a man staring at her so hard that she felt compelled to change seats. As the ever-sensational *Lincolnshire Chronicle* reported, the stranger kept looking at her until eventually he managed to catch her eye, then exclaimed, "I'm the man!" Sarah recognised her lover's voice and 'after fainting, gave expression to her great joy. In a few days they were married, and Carby … gave so glowing a description of Australia that he had little difficulty in persuading her to accompany him to the land of gold'. Robert, now 13, was on board with them, getting to know his father.

John Noble, however, was leaving his young wife behind. Anne Ray was the youngest daughter of a wealthy stonemason in the port of Whitehaven, 120 miles up the coast from Liverpool. Her father's papers suggest that he had cut her out of his will for marrying Noble, and her elder sister, Mary, seems to have been the only member of her family to witness their wedding on 17 August 1853. Anne was 22, John slightly older at 28 and temporarily land-bound while the *Tayleur* was being built. In the squat but beautiful Holy Trinity Church they said their vows and both signed the register in flowing script. Anne was literate, well-educated for a woman of her time, while John had excellent prospects and was able to provide for his wife and the family they might have in the future. Despite losing her inheritance, Anne could expect a comfortable existence as she waited for her husband to return home on the *Tayleur*, as well as the glamour and social clout of being the wife of a successful and highly celebrated master mariner.

This voyage was to be the highlight of Captain Noble's career, but the strain weighed heavily upon him. The *Tayleur*'s design had been changed partway through the construction process, the masts repositioned too far apart, leaving her unbalanced and potentially difficult to handle. Instead of having 'a pair of highly-finished oscillating engines' in addition to sails, she was powered entirely by a vast expanse of canvas, so it was even more important to have the masts accurately positioned. She also now had what Noble referred to as a 'patent rudder', which was too small to allow the ship to safely change direction. If the wind was strong it could fill her sails and rush the *Tayleur* along with the rudder acting as an inintended brake and preventing smooth sailing. Her design was innovative, but untested. As with most ships of the time, she hadn't undergone a sea trial, and as Captain Noble had not been the one to lead her down the river, he was not yet aware of how well she handled.

But with the public buoyed up by the hype surrounding the Gold Rush, and pressure from his employers to get the *Tayleur* out to sea as soon as possible, there was no time for Captain Noble to properly address any concerns. He did, however, check and double-check the compass arrangements on the enormous ship. Her compasses had been fitted by the company owned by John Gray, the leading compass manufacturer in the area, and were positioned in front of the poop, by the skylight, and near the wheel. Noble also arranged for one to be fixed by a mast as it was 'the only place in which I could find there was no deviation'. Compasses work on magnetic principles; deviation meant instead of showing north, the hand would indicate a false north, which could potentially lead a captain to steer blind. Without a reliable compass, the vessel could become lost at sea or run aground on sandbanks or rocks. Small magnets fitted beside the compass apparatus enabled the compass to compensate and read true. Noble was unhappy with the compasses but felt he could not interfere as Gray had 'more experience in compasses having deviation than any other person in this port'. Gray later stated that he had used the same principles when adjusting the compasses on the *Tayleur* as in nearly 400 other iron vessels, and that he thought the other owners were satisfied with his work. He also mentioned that the *Tayleur*'s compasses were the same as 'those supplied to Her Majesty's yacht'.

Noble was concerned, but he was in an impossible situation. The owners had paid for the foremost expert in the field to fit the compasses for their revolutionary ship, who checked and re-checked them as the *Tayleur* lay safely in the Mersey and pronounced everything in order.

John Thomas Townson, Examiner in Navigation, had assessed Captain Noble for his ordinary and extra master's certificates a few years earlier. He now discussed the compasses with Noble as the *Tayleur* lay in the port. He later commented 'I never met with any captain in Liverpool who took so much trouble with his compasses as Captain Noble did'.

Noble had sailed across the world several times. He knew from experience that once out on the open ocean without a landmark in sight, it was easy to lose your bearings. Without clear skies and visible horizons, a ship could veer off course and into trouble very quickly. A functioning compass was an essential piece of kit, and Noble wasn't convinced that the three on board the *Tayleur* would work once they put out to sea.

Indeed, the Liverpool Marine Board reported that Captain Noble 'took great pains to check the compasses', obtaining compasses from other makers, and experimenting with them while the ship was moved from dock to dock in the Mersey to see whether a compass would read true at any other position on board. Unfortunately it would not. Around 650 people were about to set sail across the Irish Sea on a ship without a reliable compass.

Chapter Four

In the tropical regions we saw the most brilliant sunsets which the imagination could conceive. Not only did they surpass those of England in degree of beauty, but they were wholly different, both as to the colouring and the form of the clouds. Sometimes the whole concave would present an intense peach blossom colour, with a band round the horizon; and on one occasion the sea reflected a rich purple, with the sky above as I have related.

The moon was sometimes almost as bright as the sun; but I was most interested on two or three occasions when the heavens were pitchy dark all over. It was then that the sea itself gave light; millions and millions of phosphoric sparks, rising like stars from the water, the ship ploughing her way through an apparent gulph [gulf] of flame. I have read print on deck solely by the aid of this phosphoric light, which has been so powerfully developed, or reflected, by the fishes in the water, that they might be seen swimming about of calm nights, twenty feet deep by our side, glowing a bright blue, as if masses of burning brimstone.

(J.H. Barrow, *Bradford Observer*, 5 January 1854)

Thursday 19 January 1854,
Mersey Bay

When the *Tayleur* left Liverpool the weather was cool and fresh but bright, boding well for the day ahead. As one passenger, William Thompson, the son of a Liverpool city councillor, remarked, 'We sailed ... with every prospect at the time of a safe and prosperous voyage'. He had chosen his ship on the recommendation of his brother, who had recently travelled with Captain Noble. Six months earlier William had been a passenger on the *Condor*, when it had caught fire 800 miles away from land. A French ship had rescued all aboard and taken them to the nearest major port, in Brazil. He had already had one lucky escape and was not looking to take any chances on the long voyage to Australia. A metal ship sounded relatively fireproof.

Captain Noble and Dr Cunningham, the ship's surgeon, walked amongst the passengers and crew, reassuring the nervous and comforting the queasy, exuding a welcome air of confidence. But all was not as well as it seemed. John Nicholls of Cawsand Bay, Devonshire joined the ship at Liverpool as a passenger and found the crew so 'inefficient' that it took four hours and several passengers' help just to raise the anchors and allow the ship to leave dock. This was but a taste of the trouble to come.

All the passengers, save those luxuriating in the first class accommodation, now clustered on deck, avoiding the ropes still coiled there, fresh from their manufacturers. They were counted, their names checked with a roll call, while an officer and several crewmen checked every berth for stowaways, using masked lanterns on long poles to shine light into any nook or cranny that could hold a body.

Robert Davison, a seaman travelling as a passenger from Deal in Kent, later recalled: 'Like all new ships she was then in great confusion. She was a new ship; when I went on board the riggers had not done with her; everything was new in her'. This newness was a problem. The ropes that made up the rigging and operated the sails were too new to pull through the blocks (a flat kind of pulley the ropes ran through to increase their mechanical power or keep their ends tidy). Davison noted that the rope had been 'stretched in cold weather, and there had been no warm weather from that time until she went to sea, so it was liable to swell again … I afterwards lent a hand to pull some of it, and some of it was very hard'.

Also James Codd, a passenger from Dublin, noted that the *Tayleur* 'received some slight injury' as she left the dock. According to the somewhat excitable *Manchester Courier and Lancashire General Advertiser*, he 'made the following prophetic remark to his companion: "I hope nothing wrong will happen to the vessel during her voyage, for do you not remember the very same thing occurred to the last vessel that was lost, and I trust it is not a bad omen?"'

The great ship was towed past the grey granite dockers' clock, its six-sided tower allowing sailors and passengers to adjust their time-pieces as they approached the docks or waved farewell with hats and handkerchiefs. The *Tayleur* drew away from the crowded buildings and windmills on the coast, out to a clear area of sea, where the air was even colder. The smell of the close-packed town faded, while the strong brine left unaccustomed eyes smarting and noses sniffling. They passed the quarantine stations where many sailors and incoming passengers had died of cholera, dysentery and yellow fever before reaching shore. The once great man o'war ships were now bare of masts and roofed over to allow diseases to ravage weakened bodies away from the thronging masses of Liverpool, or let old sailors live in peace away from the mainland. The sea lapped at the sides of these vessels as they watched the iron clipper sail by.

The swell of the open sea would have been an unwelcome sensation to passengers and crew on the ocean for the first time, and those prone to seasickness. It took a while for the apprentices and some of the stewards to find their sea-legs. Many of the passengers lay prone in their berths below deck, while others watched above as the mainland dimmed in the distance and twilight fell. Some were wearing all the clothes they owned, layers of coats and shirts, undergarments and trousers keeping them warm, if a little uncomfortable.

A few of the passengers wore money belts around their waists, like James Wood, a weaver from Delph in Yorkshire. According to E.J. Bourke, Wood may have been a veteran of the Californian Gold Rush a few years earlier, and carried his money in a packet strapped to his waist. It would have weighed heavy on his hips, but this was probably the most secure option for a passenger. Some of the women had their cash sewn into their undergarments, including one lady who, unbeknownst to her fellow passengers, had £3,000 secreted in her corsets and stays. This would not have been obvious to anyone else, except the maid lacing her into her underwear.

Mid-Victorian women wore up to 16 layers of clothing, including bloomers, stockings, garters, chemise (undershirt), corset, a corset cover (like a fitted shirt), the hooped frame for a crinoline skirt, petticoats (several would be worn in cooler weather) and a near floor-length skirt, a blouse, high-necked under a long-sleeved bodice with a long row of tiny buttons (buttonhooks were commonly used) or hooks and eyes, a jacket, and a shawl or mantle (a cape-like garment worn over the shoulders). Women and girls from the lower classes usually wore petticoats stiffened with quilting, or sewed a tube stiffened with horsehair near the hem of their skirt in place of an expensive hooped frame. The natural outline of a woman's body was distorted by the whale-boned rigours of their undergarments and the voluminous bell-shaped crinoline skirts popular at the time. A few extra layers of paper and gold would make little difference to the bulky formal curve visible to their fellow travellers.

While passengers who owned watches checked the time and women pulled their shawls tighter against the wind, Captain Noble discussed the *Tayleur*'s compasses with John Corren, a branch pilot who guided ships through the channels near the port until they were safely out to sea. Corren observed small differences between the compasses on board, but not enough to warrant them turning back. The *Tayleur* continued to be towed by the *Victory*, the little steamer chugging noisily across the water, smoke trailing in its wake as the enormous clipper towered over it. Corren had worked as a branch pilot for two decades and was well accustomed to the antics of passengers and crew when ships set off on long voyages. His later remark, 'I thought that some of the crew were not what they pretended to be', suggests that all was not quite as it should have been on board the *Tayleur*.

The crew raised the sails, the newer seamen requiring instruction, and the wind filled them easily. With wind came speed, and the steamer had to move alongside the *Tayleur* to avoid being crushed by the enormous hull 'as such was the sailing qualities of the ship that she would have run over the steamer'. Although he noticed 'half a point difference between the compasses below and those upon deck', the pilot admired the ship. He later praised her, noting that she 'answered her helm and steered like a fish and I do not hesitate to state that I believed her to be the fastest ship afloat. When a breeze sprung up and the sails were set, by the steam tug's capacity which I knew to be ten knots per hour, I found that the ship was leaving her at the rate of three or four miles an hour, thus making the speed of the ship from 18 to 14 knots an hour'.

A knot is a unit of speed used to measure the time taken to travel one nautical mile, the equivalent to 1.15 miles on land. The *Tayleur* was cutting through the sea at between 16 and 20 miles an hour; quite an impressive speed for people accustomed to travelling on foot or in a horse and cart. Her crisp white sails billowed with wind, ropes snapping against the fixtures. With sailing ships like the *Tayleur*, wind brings speed but also waves and an unusual rocking motion unlike anything to be experienced on land.

A while later James McLellan, a Canadian crewman, found that their speed brought problems, 'we were obliged to shorten sail; in fact she became unmanageable'. As the majority of the crew were well fed and rested before they set out to sea, this was not a good sign, but was hardly surprising given how thick and stretchy the ropes were, and how difficult they were to handle and move through the blocks and pulleys.

On their last night in port, a few of the crew had gone ashore and taken advantage of their final hours of freedom. Much to the annoyance of Captain Noble, the more inebriated men had then sneaked below decks and hidden in the passengers' quarters, or climbed the rigging and tied themselves into the sails far above the hubbub on deck, the swaying of the masts rocking them to sleep. In the chaos of the *Tayleur* and the *Victory* preparing to go their separate ways, their absence was noticed by the crew, Captain Noble, and some of the seafaring passengers, who started muttering to one another. The clerks and friends of some of the passengers, who had travelled to bid farewell to loved ones they might never see again, now called their goodbyes as the tow ropes slipped through the water and were hauled up on deck. People cheered and cried, waving farewell as the *Tayleur* took off into the dark and the *Victory* steamed towards the rain-dimmed lights of Liverpool.

But not all the passengers were where they should have been either. The pilot later recalled:

An extraordinary circumstance took place when the steam tug came up to the ship to take those parties on shore who had gone out to see their friends off, together with the clerks from the office who were on board. An Irishman, a passenger in the confusion and noise that occurred when the steamer went alongside the ship, thought something was radically wrong and for self-preservation he jumped on board the tug. It was quite dark at the time the tug left the ship and when the steamer had proceeded some distance on her course toward Liverpool, someone observed a person standing on the paddle box and said to him "Come down out of that", to which he replied in amazement, "Where are we going to" and they told him the steamer was going to Liverpool. He appeared to be dreadfully confused and said he wanted to go to Melbourne. The steamer was then put about, with a view to putting him on board the ship, but she was going too fast that we could not catch her, and the man was therefore brought to Liverpool as he stood, leaving his clothes and all he had on board – an accident to him, but one which probably saved his life.

Chapter Five

Sometime between 12 and 2 I awoke with a start, caused by a loud and violent booming blow, followed by a rush of water which came dashing down the main hatchway, and flooding all the 'tween decks, every cabin inclusive. A lurch instantly followed, which sent all the water swosh over to the other side of the ship, but this seemed only done to give a more vehement impulse to the counter-lurch on our side, the roll of which went to such an extent lower and lower that I thought this time at last we must go clean over, and ... down came rushing in our low-sunken side an avalanche of all the moveable contents of the entire 'tween decks – cooking tins and crockery, washing things, all loose articles of every description, with boxes, jars, and tubs, and kegs and cabin furniture bursting away from their fastenings, through cabin doors, and bringing many cabin doors and panels along with them, together with the heavy crashing hatchway ladders – in one tremendous avalanche, cataract, and chaos, like the total destruction and end of all things.

(Unnamed emigrant's account of the wrecking of the *Rodneyrig*,
published in the *Morning Post*, 6 September 1853)

**Thursday 19 January 1854,
The Irish Sea**

It was dark now, and the yellow glow of covered lights on the *Victory* soon disappeared across the waves, leaving the *Tayleur* alone on the surging swell of the sea. The wind picked up again, filling the canvas and hastening the clipper across the waves. Although the ship responded to the men at the helm, the crew found it impossible to manage the sails, and before they could tie up the larger ones, reducing the area of canvas available to the wind, one split.

One of the 111 Irish passengers aboard, Robert Holland, who was a confident and wealthy man, knew 'something of nautical affairs' and owned two yachts. Holland said later that he 'did not go to bed that night in consequence of seeing the ship was not properly handled'. He described the chaotic state of the crew, saying:

I saw some of the sails clewed up [rolled up] and others flapping; the mizzen topsail and the main top sail [two of the larger sails; each of the Tayleur's *three masts had three large sails] were torn. I assisted, myself, in endeavouring to furl and clew up those sails as I saw that the men were not capable of doing it, and thinking my services were sadly wanting. I do not think there were enough hands aboard to manage the ship as she was at the time, it might do well if there were a steady breeze.*

Some of the passengers retreated from the cold, damp air above deck to their cabins and berths and the long wooden tables in the common areas below. Despite its weight the ship followed the violent movement of the rolling waves, inflicting nausea and sickness on the passengers and some of the crew. There were a couple of flush toilets available, but most of those affected would have kept a tight grip on their chamber pots or slop buckets, and hoped that a friend or family member would empty it over the side later. Steward Charles Griffiths was kept busy with the sick passengers, while his wife and their baby, Arthur, settled into their own quarters.

Passengers on the *Tayleur* and other emigrant ships would have had some idea of what to expect on board before setting out on their journey. Newspapers regularly printed accounts from passengers with sage words of advice and warnings against rogues and scoundrels in the ports. Books like the comprehensive *The Immigrant's Guide To Australia*, published by John Capper in 1853, laid out the rules most passenger ships dictated to their customers in accordance with the legislation of the time. A version of this guide was usually pinned throughout the passenger decks. Aimed at keeping the ship safe from fire or explosions, deterring flies and vermin, and keeping the air clean and dry, they also attempted to discourage the passengers and crew from getting into mischief. If there was a disagreement among the travellers then those involved still had to live in close quarters for the next few weeks. Capper's guide emphasised the importance of cleanliness and routine on board ship for passengers and crew:

With the view of promoting order and health on board passenger ships the following rules have been put in order:

1. *Every passenger to rise at 7 am unless otherwise permitted by the surgeon, or, if no surgeon, the master.*
2. *Breakfast from 8 to 9 am, dinner at 1 pm, supper at 6 pm.*
3. *The passengers to be in their beds at 10 pm.*
4. *Fires to be lighted by the passengers' cook at 7 am, and kept alight by him till 7 pm, then to be extinguished, unless otherwise directed by the master or required for the use of the sick.*
5. *The master to determine the order in which the passengers shall be entitled to the use of the fires for cooking. The cook to take care that this order is preserved.*
6. *Three safety lamps to be lit at dusk, one to be kept burning all night in the main hatchway, the two others may be extinguished at 10 pm.*
7. *No naked light to be allowed at any time or on any account.*
8. *The passengers, when dressed, to roll up their beds [bedding], to sweep the decks (including the space under the bottom of the berths), and to throw the dirt overboard.*
9. *Breakfast not to commence till this is done.*
10. *The sweepers for the day to be taken in rotation from the males above 14, in the proportion of five for every 100 passengers.*
11. *Duties of the sweepers to be to clean the ladders, hospitals, and roundhouses, to sweep the decks after every meal, and to dry holystone [rub the deck with blocks of a particularly soft pale sandstone, the smaller blocks being called 'prayer books' and the larger ones 'bibles'] and scrape them after breakfast.*
12. *But the occupant of each berth to see that his own berth is well brushed out, and single women are to keep their own compartment clean in ships where a separate compartment is allotted to them.*
13. *The beds to be well shaken and aired on deck and the bottom boards, if not fixtures, to be removed and dry-scrubbed and taken on deck at least twice a week.*

14. *Two days in the week to be appointed by the master as washing days, but no clothes to be washed or dried between decks.*
15. *The coppers and cooking vessels to be cleaned every day.*
16. *The scuttles and stern ports, if any, to be kept open (weather permitting) from 7 am to 10 pm, and the hatches at all hours.*
17. *Hospitals to be established, with an area, in ships carrying 100 passengers, of not less than 48 superficial feet, with two or four bed-berths; and in ships carrying 200 passengers, of not less than 100 superficial feet, with six bed-berths.*
18. *On Sunday the passengers to be mustered at 10 am, when they will be expected to appear in clean and decent apparel. The day to be observed as religiously as circumstances will permit.*
19. *No spirits or gunpowder to be taken on board by any passenger. Any that may be discovered to be taken into the custody of the master till the expiration of the voyage.*
20. *No loose hay or straw to be allowed below.*
21. *No smoking to be allowed between decks.*
22. *All gambling, fighting, riotous or quarrelsome behaviour, swearing and violent language, to be at once put a stop to. Swords and other offensive weapons, as soon as the passengers embark, to be placed in the custody of the master.*
23. *No sailors to remain on the passenger deck among the passengers except on duty.*
24. *No passenger to go to the ship's cookhouse without special permission from the master, nor to remain in the forecastle among the sailors on any account.*

Captain Noble ran a tight ship, and these rules would most likely have been adhered to without any threats of cruelty on his part. But once the daily round of cleaning, airing and eating was done with, the passengers had a lot of time on their hands. There was very little for the passengers to do on the voyage, especially those who had brought their servants along to facilitate their life in a new world.

To prevent boredom, ship passengers were advised to keep journals, skip or climb rigging to keep fit, or make a ball from rags to play with. Those with an interest in scrimshaw whittled cleaned meat bones into salt cellars, walking-stick handles and mementoes. Seamen and passengers on ships of the time carved dice and dominoes and discreetly gambled their time away, or played chequers and draughts. The noise of blade on bone would have scarcely been audible over the groans of the seasick confined to their trough beds. A plank at the side separated people from their neighbours and prevented the occupants from rolling to the floor with every heave of the ship. While Dr Cunningham's wife, children and servant were getting used to their cabin berths after the comforts of the family estate in Fife, the ship's surgeon moved through the different classes of compartment. His senses would have been assaulted by the stink of vomit mingling with fresh paint and brine, as the lanterns threw shadows, distorting his vision.

Some of the passengers, especially those with nautical experience, flaunted the rules and stayed above deck to watch the captain and crew at work and savour the night air. Robert Holland was one of them, 'I mixed amongst the crew myself continually and I found that a number of them were foreigners. I spoke to several of them frequently myself but they could not understand me nor I them'. This was common at the time, as many ships had a multi-national crew, but some of the passengers would only ever have encountered people from their own home towns before setting off to Liverpool to board the *Tayleur*, so this proved to be a subject of discussion for many. There were concerns voiced amongst the passengers, too, about the language barrier between members of the crew. Most could understand English, a lot could speak it, but as Robert Davison, a passenger and sailor from Kent, felt, 'in moments of danger it is of great importance that men should know the orders given to them'.

Robert Holland was growing increasingly anxious on deck, and shared Davison's concerns. They were still only a few hours from port:

On Thursday night my apprehensions were so excited from the manner in which I saw the ship handled, and the rapid pace we were going through the water, and the great confusion there was on deck, I went into the second cabin and called some of my friends, as I dreaded we might go on the Irish coast, which I thought was to leeward. I said to these people I thought there was danger, and urged them to come up; some of them said they would be of no use on deck; at this time I saw the captain on the quarter deck; I considered we were in great danger at the time; the ropes were new and the blocks were too small for them to run through, at least the ropes would not run freely through them; at one time I saw a sailor having to go aloft to grease some of the ropes in order to lift the main top sail. I observed that difficulty on Thursday night, and I heard the sailors cursing the riggers for the condition they had sent them to sea in.

The first mate, 27-year-old Michael Murphy of Wexford, Ireland, gave a slightly different account, and since it was dark and noisy on deck, the crew may have had a more accurate idea of events than the passengers. The half-gale was too much for the amount of canvas they had open to it. The crew shortened the sails from 8 pm until 4 am – eight hours of difficult work in the rainy darkness, taking much longer than would usually be necessary according to passengers with nautical knowledge. But as Chief Mate Murphy recalled, 'the reef tackle blocks and some of the gear got foul. And the canvas being new it was very difficult to handle. We split the maintopsail … and reefed the torn part in'.

But William K. Badcock, a first class passenger and a sailor with nine years' experience, judged that 'the crew were totally incompetent to manage the ship'. He described their shortcomings in detail:

The mate could not get anyone to go on the yards to shorten sail and the ship was at the mercy of the wind and the sea. Some idea of the incompetence of the crew may be formed when it is known that it took nearly three hours to take in the mizzen topsail and neither the maintopsail nor the lower sails could be got in at all. We, however, struggled through the night, our sails flapping and beating in a frightening manner. The boatswain and the third mate exerted themselves a great deal but the men did not appear to know their work. It immediately began to be whispered about that we would never reach the end of our voyage the crew being a mixed medley of many nations having an imperfect acquaintance with the English language and subsequently being unable to understand the captain's orders.

That same night another ship, the *Scotland*, was in distress in the roiling waves of the Irish Sea. As a passenger on the steam-packet *Prince* recollected:

[*Captain*] *Dearl received orders on Wednesday night, January 18, to return to Dublin from Liverpool as soon as the tide permitted. We had been at sea some twelve hours, when Mr Dearl was struck by the strange sailing of the* Scotland, *and soon came to the conclusion that she had no rudder. He bore down to her, ascertained that she wanted assistance, and at once prepared, at great risk both to his person and vessel, to pass to her ropes, by means of which to take her in tow.*

The wind was blowing a gale at the time; and, from the position of the Scotland, *added to which, in consequence of having struck on the Kish bank, water was rapidly increasing in her hold, it seemed that had Mr Dearl not succeeded in bringing her up she must inevitably [go] ashore, in which case, from the nature of things (by-the-bye, she had no life-boat), what must have become of her crew? [Adequate provision of lifeboats was an exception rather than a rule.]*

It was very disheartening, after having borne down to her the third time, to have the towing rope broken. Impressed, however, with the peril of those awaiting his assistance, our captain nobly made fresh attempts to attach the helpless vessel this time on the leeward side, but the ropes again gave way, and the remainder of the night of Thursday was consumed in preparations for again taking her in tow.

Miles to the east, passengers on the *Tayleur* listened to the wind and the rain beating down on the deck above, and the waves battering her metal sides. The iron clipper 'had struggled through the night with her sails flapping and beating about in a frightening manner'. As Captain Walker, an experienced sailor, reported afterwards: 'It must be taken into consideration that the *Tayleur* had only been about twelve hours from port. The running rigging and sails were new, and of course more difficult to work than they would have been after being in use for a little time; the officers and crew were strangers to each other – generally the case at the commencement of the voyage'.

But a sense of unease had already spread through the passengers. 'At about 4 o'clock on the Friday morning, I was lying in my berth with my clothes on, when a passenger named Holland told me that there was great confusion on board and that if any accident occurred I would have the best chance of saving myself by being on deck', remembered Michael Reidy, a wealthy passenger from County Galway.

A steerage passenger, Thomas Willet, saw one of the crew climb down from the rigging and remark to the third mate, "If you have no better men to send up to assist me than those, I shall stay down and do no more for they can neither understand what I say, nor do they know their duty". The third mate agreed to send up two more men, who climbed the freshly strung ropes in the wind and the rain with little light to see by. A short while later Captain Noble ordered the third mate to climb the rigging and see what was going on. According to Willet, when the mate came back he told the captain, "There are three or four of those beggars lashed to the top asleep". Captain Noble apparently replied: "If [I catch] them sleeping they [will] recollect the time".

William Thompson, travelling first class with Captain Noble on the recommendation of his brother, was disappointed. 'The officers and the captain were attentive to the ship, although to me, there appeared to be some deficiency with regard to the crew. The captain himself said that out of the whole crew he could muster only fifteen sailors'. And John Nicholls, an old sailor from Devonshire, travelling as a passenger, commented on 'the weakness of the crew', and how 'the sails were always flapping about and would have been knocked to pieces had the canvas not been new'. About eight o'clock on Friday morning Nicholls heard the captain reprimand one of the crew, telling him "you could not be got up last night my customer", and he also noticed the strength of the wind throughout the day.

Across the water, the *Scotland* was still in trouble. The ship was close to the mainland, but might as well have been in the middle of the ocean as no help could be obtained. Captain Dearl, unable to lash the stricken vessel to the side of the *Prince*, ordered towing ropes to be attached to the *Scotland*. An anonymous passenger aboard the *Prince* told the *Freeman's Journal*, 'This is my first voyage, and the last time I desire to hear men cry "Don't leave us to perish"'. The ships pitched in the swell as the *Scotland* drifted closer to the shore. The passenger heard the crew shout "Man the lifeboat", as the wind buffeted the ships, rocking them up and down on the huge waves, spray dashing the decks and the men working to save the *Scotland*. Eventually, the sound of the pumps working to drain the excess water was heard above the wind, and Captain Dearl agreed to stay beside the *Scotland* for the night.

But the damaged ship drifted from her position. Dearl and the captain of the *Albert*, a large steamer that had arrived in search of the long overdue *Scotland*, could not tow her to harbour. As the anonymous passenger later explained:

[*With*] *the unfortunate and ill-starred crew placed in imminent danger … she drifted ashore. Her masts [were] felled, with hope of keeping her afloat, or permitting her to be washed higher up on the beach. In the meanwhile our lifeboat and that of the other steamer happily were enabled to make the wreck, and, as was afterwards ascertained, rescue from certain death those of the ship's company who had remained on board, in all some 22 persons. The crew originally, I understand, consisted of 25, besides whom there were some fishermen on board … Throughout the whole affair (to me a most exciting scene) the conduct and exertions of the captain and crew of the* Prince *were most praiseworthy.*

However, Captain Dearl would not have much time to rest before his services were called on by another ship.

Chapter Six

We have seen the usual marine prodigies. Huge whales we frequently met with, and one vast fellow took it into his head to cross our bows so close, that the sailors thought we should run into him. Porpoises we encountered in shoals; one, weighing about 130 pounds, we caught with a harpoon. His flesh tasted something like bullock's kidney, and it was greedily devoured.

In the warmer latitudes we saw shoals of those beautiful little creatures, the flying fish. They only rise a few yards from the water, and seldom keep on the wing – or more properly speaking, on the fin – for a longer distance than a couple of hundred yards. Then they plunge in the water, and as soon as they have wetted their fins, rise again, as they can only fly whilst the fin continues wet. The most pitiful part of the business is, that their flight, so beautiful to the spectator, is to the poor fishes – a flight for life; being caused by the pursuit of their insatiable enemies, the dolphins and benitos [tuna], by whom they are devoured in thousands. These huntsmen of the deep can swim as fast as their victims fly, and generally follow them in their flight, so that when the little creatures dip into water, the voracious maws of their enemies are open to receive them. The flying fish is about the size of a very small herring. A benito which we caught with a hook weighed 37 lbs.; and reflected all the colours of the rainbow as he lay on the deck.

(J.H. Barrow, *Bradford Observer*, 5 January 1854)

Friday 20 January 1854,
The Irish Sea

Throughout Friday as the wind grew stronger more people took to their berths with seasickness, and the situation aboard the *Tayleur* worsened. Michael Reidy, a second class passenger, confronted the captain – an unusual and bold move – informing him, 'The passengers [feel] deeply disappointed in the crew'. Captain Noble replied that the crew had presented themselves in Liverpool "as good and efficient men" and that he had had no way of knowing their true skills until the ship was out at sea. Now he could see they were incompetent and cared little for the state of the vessel, hiding themselves amongst the passengers below deck. Reidy recalled thinking that the crew 'were very inefficient and that no person could be justified in thinking his life safe'.

There were other hiding places for errant members of the crew, besides the passengers' berths. The Chief Mate, Michael Murphy, 'found three or four skulking in the forecastle; I reported them to the captain; I heard no complaints from the passengers about the seamen; the captain was angry about three fellows skulking; he came one time into the forecastle to beat them out with his speaking trumpet'.

Life aboard an emigrant ship was hard, even on a ship as modern as the *Tayleur*. There were no days off, no respite from the lurch and roll of the sea, and always plenty of work to be done. As in any job, some of the men were less hardworking than the rest. Hangovers and stormy weather combined to make some of the stewards and seamen particularly reluctant to assist with tasks above deck. Discipline was usually strictly enforced at sea, with physical punishment common for infractions, but Noble was not a man to dole out harsh punishments such as a whipping, even when his peers would have considered it justified.

John Aislabie and several other passengers chatted to the second mate Edward Kewley about the 'badly fixed' state of the crew, 'I said I thought we ought to put in to Liverpool, or put into some place for shelter'. Kewley explained in that case "every seaman on board will leave the ship", including himself. "There is such a scandalous crew on board that it is impossible to manage the ship in any way".

The upper deck should have been kept clear, but passengers noticed that some luggage was still sitting there, exposed to wind, rain and the froth of the sea, and had not been deposited below decks or stowed in the hold. One man commented 'The deck was covered with coils of ropes from the manufacturer', a trip-hazard for those walking or working there, and risking the ropes getting wet and swollen, making it harder for them to pass through the blocks, should they be needed later. The weather was changeable but generally foul, and the majority of the crew were working above decks, trying to tame the *Tayleur*'s wayward sails.

Captain Noble was baffled by the handling of the ship, but managed to hide his confusion from many of the passengers, with one even commenting afterwards, 'She sailed like a duck, and was the most easily steered vessel I ever saw'. The reality was that the ultra-modern iron clipper was a source of great frustration for this extremely able captain. 'She would not pay off', he explained later. 'I could assign no cause for her not paying off but was much surprised by it. She answered the helm very badly ... Another vessel would have done this work in half the time and in only half the distance'.

They were also lost. Like the pilot before him, Chief Mate Michael Murphy 'observed a difference of about half a point between two of the compasses'. The needles were no longer in agreement, despite Captain Noble's insistence on having them checked before they left port. Davison, a seaman and passenger from Kent, recalled watching the captain struggle to take 'an observation'. He continued: 'The vessel answered the helm well on the wind ... I saw the crew reefing the mizzen topsail, and it was not done in a seamanlike manner, because they were so long and went so lubberly about it. I account for it by their not being used to one another, and the canvas being new'.

Noble tried to work out their location the old-fashioned way, using a sextant (a navigational instrument that allows the user to judge the angle between a celestial object like the sun or the North Star and the horizon so they can calculate approximate locations from charts), but to no avail. 'I put it to my eyes several times but could not succeed in getting a clear horizon. If I got the sun clear I could not get an observation unless I also got a clear horizon.'

Meanwhile Hugh Cowan, third mate, spent the afternoon 'putting things into their places' with some of the crew. He recalled how on the Friday night the weather was decent enough for him to see some of the beacons along the coast, with the help of the captain:

The Calf of Man lights [were in sight at the time]. The captain showed them to me through his opera glass. It was not blowing so strong: the night was still fine ... the morning was fine and little wind ... between 10 and

11 o'clock I went aft to the poop, to give the cook his meat, and the captain told me to go to the binnacle to see how the head was. I told him; and then he went forward and found there was a difference of one point between the two compasses [twice the difference the Captain had noticed just a few hours before]. [The crew took] a long time the first night as many of them had been drinking; on the second they did their work very well.

But one of the steerage passengers, James Oldfield, recalled things differently: 'Some of the passengers who were sailors were got to work that night as the crew were not able to do what was required'. It seems odd that Noble appears to have struggled to recruit a competent and experienced crew while the *Tayleur* was moored in Liverpool, yet had so many able sailors amongst the passengers. But there were other enigmas surrounding the *Tayleur*.

* * *

That afternoon the weather improved for a short while. Instead of taking this opportunity to retire to his quarters for a rest, a wash, a change of clothes or a snatched nap in a sheltered area on deck, Noble, who had a reputation as a careful, cautious man, remained alert, watching over his men. Many captains would drink at least a shot or two of spirits, to warm themselves a little in the sea air, yet several passengers noted that Noble was 'perfectly sober'. At one point the weather was so fine that those on deck could see the stars shining in the deep blue sky, and the wind calmed enough to leave the water smooth and give the travellers a few hours' respite from the tilt and sway of the waves. A few hours later, at about 7 pm, the wind increased so fast that the men had to take in the sails once again.

Charles Lee, a passenger in second class, saw Noble leave the deck in the charge of the mate for a few minutes, as the ship slowed from eight knots to two (approximately 9 to 2.3 miles per hour). Several second class passengers voiced their frustrations to the mate, and pointed out the dangers of keeping the *Tayleur* for so long on the same tack (heading in one direction). Noble returned and overheard before the mate could answer. He was furious at this attempt to meddle with his running of the ship. 'Captain Noble said that he was the master of the ship and he would allow no man to interfere. The seaman hoped that he had not made any remark that was impertinent but as there were a great many passengers on board and as he was one of them, he had a duty to perform. Captain Noble made no remark but turned away'.

The passengers returned to their quarters below decks; when they rose in the dark at 7 am on Saturday morning the *Tayleur* was still on the same tack. They tried to raise their concerns with the captain, only for him to ignore them once again. John Frazer, the ship's carpenter, was a trusted member of the crew who had travelled with Noble on the *Australia* the year before. '[Captain Noble] ordered me to get fresh compasses up ... on Saturday morning ... between eight and nine o'clock. He said "Carpenter I believe the compasses are incorrect; the one in the binnacle and that at the fore part of the poop are different"'.

Frazer tinkered with them, but even if this had solved the problem of magnetic interference from the iron ship, the compasses could only reveal the direction the ship was now heading in – not their current position. The correct procedure would have been for Captain Noble to sound the depths. This involved a member of the crew casting a line overboard with a lead weight or 'plummet' attached to the end, the line marked with fathoms to allow a depth to be found. This depth would then be compared to known depth measurements on a navigation chart, allowing the crew of a lost ship to work out its probable position. Noble told either the second or third mate to prepare the lead, and was informed when it was ready, but for some reason he did not give the order to use it.

John Nicholls, an old sailor from Devonshire, travelling on the *Tayleur* as a passenger, said:

> [*The* Tayleur] *was tolerably quick until about daybreak on Saturday morning. When my fellow passenger Ryder, who had been on deck, came down, and I asked him what they were doing on deck; he said the weather was fine and the captain was making sail, and the ship was laying her course down channel. I asked him how her head was; he said he had not looked at the compass, but one of the sailors told him she was going WSW. I said that is not the course down the channel but more likely to fetch Dublin, and if the wind backs against the sun, he, the captain would be very glad to take it in again.*

I longed to speak to the captain, for I considered we had been too long on the port tack, but I thought I should interfere with his duty if I did so. I suppose we were going six or seven knots then, for there was not a very heavy sea on ... I suppose we could see about three or four miles, the captain was walking on the round house and appeared to look anxiously under the lee of the spanker [one of the sails at the rear of the ship] as if he expected to see land.

Now experiencing a 'heavy rolling sea', the passengers were tossed about below decks; hurled against walls and tables as the *Tayleur* pitched up and down on the massive waves. They would have been bruised, sickened, and in some cases terrified. For most, this was unlike anything they had faced before. But, not all were disturbed. At about 11 am a passenger called Willet and a companion were up on deck watching waves 'rolling mountains high' and 'admiring the hills and valleys made in the water by the storm'.

Captain Noble was growing tense; something wasn't right. James McLellan, a 26-year-old crewman originally from Canada, was sent by one of the officers to work the deep sea lead at the rear of the ship. 'The captain said to me "Be very particular with that lead for I want to use it shortly." Well they had shortened sail and everything and I had the lead line finished [he had prepared a line 100 fathoms long], I said "Captain Noble it stands at a hundred fathoms." "I suppose that will do", he said, "you lay forward and haul down the jib [triangular sail at the very front of the ship]"'.

At the same time seasoned sailor John Nicholls was helping out below decks, despite his status as passenger. 'In consequence of some of the stewards being sick I was asked to assist in getting up the provisions for the passengers' dinner, and went to the hold to do so. I had been down about half an hour when Henry Horrow, a fellow passenger from Devonport, came down and said "John, there is land close on her lee [the side closest to shore, when a wind is blowing the ship towards shore]". I heard the ropes running upon deck, and said to the purser "I'll go up on deck and see what is going on".

As the weather grew ever more dire, all hands rushed to shorten the sails, and one crewman later said: 'it was very boisterous and it blowed as if it would take the masts out of her'. A passenger said '[The Captain was] quite steady and sober and dressed in a blue overcoat. I saw him occasionally looking out. At eleven o'clock I saw him looking intently over the starboard bow'.

Then sailor James McLellan clambered along the front of the ship, careful not to fall into the heaving waves below, hauled down the jib and cried "Land-ho on the lee bow!"

Chapter Seven

In a word [the Tayleur] *is an amazing vessel and the workmanship in her is throughout of the very best description. With respect to her model, it is all that could be wished for in a vessel built to combine sailing qualities with large enough space for the accommodation of passengers. She is slightly hollow in her entrance, and sharp astern, with an ample floor, which will enable her to carry a large spread of canvas. There is thus every certainty that she will prove at once a fast sailer and a safe and comfortable vessel.*

(*The Illustrated London News*, 26 November 1853)

Saturday 21 January 1854,
The Irish Sea

The *Tayleur* was now being swept towards land at a rate of about two and a half to three knots (the rate of a fast walk). This would have felt much faster to those on deck since the land was now looming ever closer and the sea increasingly rough. The winter wind caught the rest of the sails, their ropes jammed and fouled around the rigging and masts, preventing the crew from reefing the canvas in as she sped nearer to the unexpected land mass rising black and dangerous from the sea.

The tide was running inwards, carrying her closer to the rocks and stopping the crew from turning her onto another course away from the cliffs. Two seamen at a time hauled the wheel hard, trying to shift the stubborn helm, and turn the 'patented rudder' which Captain Noble had worried was too small. But the iron clipper couldn't come about; no matter what the men tried she would *not* turn into the wind and away from the cliffs. Those below decks were thrown about, battered into their berths, luggage, and the long wooden tables laid out for their lunch. Some passengers rushed above decks, while many lay prone in their bunks, too seasick to move, as vomit spilled from slop buckets and chamber pots rolled about. The mugs and cutlery hanging from hooks directly above their beds would have clattered to the floor or fallen onto the unfortunate occupants caught in their blankets below.

Those with experience of the sea were at an advantage, and better able to cope with the constant rolling motion of the deck below their feet. Sailor Robert Davison was travelling from Kent to Australia in second class. He heard a cry of "Land on the bow" at about 10.40 am. 'I saw the land about a mile and a half distant', he recalled later:

> *It was then blowing what was just a good stiff breeze for a large vessel like the* Tayleur, *and the weather was very hazy, with slight showers of rain now and then coming very thick. The captain was on deck at the time, from the time I left Liverpool until the time I heard the cry "Land ahead" it never occurred to me that there was danger; it was the least of my thoughts. Some of the passengers expressed their apprehension, but I told them that matters were only as they usually were in a new ship at the commencement of a voyage.*

Thomas Kemp was in his first class cabin below deck when another passenger ran in and warned him of the impending disaster. Kemp raced up the wooden steps, and was horrified to see land less than a mile away. 'I saw there was no hope of escape, and I prepared myself for the worst. As soon as it was known to passengers that land was so close they all crowded on deck, and caused such confusion that the crew were prevented from obeying any orders that might have been conveyed to them by the officers'.

The ship sailed on, moving inexorably towards the rocks rising 'like a mountain in the middle of the sea', as Coroner Henry Davis would later describe them. Captain Noble was doing his best to give orders to the crew, bellowing through a metal speaking trumpet so they would hear him over the screams of the passengers and roar of the wind and sea. He then gathered the male passengers about him and shouted, "If you want to preserve your lives you must come to these ropes and assist the seamen". A steerage passenger, 21-year-old John Ryder, took a dim view of Noble's actions, saying that the crew 'had not the least control over the ship. They were unable to hoist a sail without the help of the passengers [who are] a rough lot, fit for any rascally deed. The crew were worse than women'. Rascally or not, they did their best to prevent the tragedy about to unfold.

Robert Davison and some other men tried to wrestle the sails into position, hoping to allow the ship to slow down and clear the rocks, 'but the sheet got off the belaying pin [shaped like a porridge spurtle or club, and used to tether the ropes used to bind the sail in place], and took possession of the whole [lot] of us, knocked two or three men down and obliged us to haul it down again. The captain immediately sung out "Let go the anchor" and ran forward to superintend the doing of it. [The ship] was drifting dead on shore'.

Some of the men employed on the *Tayleur* did rise to the occasion, such as Captain Noble and Dr Cunningham. Others behaved in a less heroic fashion, including an unnamed steward who wrestled a life-preserver away from the passengers, and kept it for himself. Yet the actions of the ship surgeon stood out amidst the trauma. His position on the ship had already made him a familiar face to the travellers; now his selflessness drew their attention and lodged in their memories. The *Hereford Times* later reported, along with many other newspapers, 'Dr Cunningham was seen everywhere trying to restore confidence and courage amongst the passengers and endeavouring to preserve order and coolness'. Dr Cunningham's wife Susan comforted the two little boys while their father helped those on board. Some passengers still sat below deck, unaware of the danger they were in. Cunningham spread the word and sought out other composed individuals to aid him in calming the passengers.

This helped some of those thronging the deck, although many shared the thoughts of Robert Holland who said, 'when I saw the land I knew nothing could save her'. William Thompson, a passenger, was sitting in the cabin reading a newspaper when he 'heard a scuffling on deck and an apparent confusion, but this did not at the time cause me to entertain any uneasiness, as I knew we were about to wear ship [change direction]. A short time afterwards my attention was further attracted by hearing the people on deck crying out in a state of great alarm "we are going to be lost, we are on a lee shore!" Those on deck seemed to be running to and fro, evidently in a state of excitement. At this moment, the surgeon of the ship Mr Cunningham came into the cabin, his countenance expressive of the keenest anxiety. When suspecting what had occurred, I said "doctor is it true that the ship is going on shore?'"

According to Thompson, the doctor replied "yes she is going on shore, and a few minutes will seal all our fates". Then:

I inquired what sort of a shore it was and he replied "a bold rocky coast and I do not think that in the event of the ship striking there any of us will be saved." He asked me to remain in the cabin (the poop cabin, at the rear of the ship) to keep the ladies as quiet as possible, that being considered the most desirable under the circumstances. There were then eight females in the cabin. I told him I should as far as possible comply with this injunction and I sat down at the cabin table where I had previously been and I did not go on deck at all at that time.

The surgeon then left us. I continued in the cabin, the females making most anxious enquiries as to what was the matter, and whether there was any danger. I endeavoured to appease their apprehensions by giving evasive answers and telling them we were wearing ship. Feeling assured that whatever the result might be, anything tending to create confusion or interfere with the management of the ship would only lessen the chances of escape from the calamity with which, at that time, we were threatened. The noise on the deck continued, and the other indications which presented themselves tended to confirm the most dismal apprehensions which the communication by the surgeon had suggested to our minds. The period was one of the most painful anxiety. The females were kept in ignorance of the real state of things for a short time longer, when it was made painfully apparent the vessel was going on shore by both anchors being let go. The shock was such as to shake the vessel from stem to stern [end to end]. No sooner were the anchors let go than the females made a rush from the cabin in a state of the utmost terror and alarm.

Noble ordered the anchors dropped intending to use their weight as a brake, which he hoped would allow the head of the ship to swing round enough to clear the rocks and skim past the cliffs looming tall and treacherous over the deck. "I had no doubt when I first saw land, that I should clear it", he later argued, "if the ship had worked properly, I should have succeeded". It very nearly worked.

'The starboard anchor was immediately let go, and it took all the chain which was on deck – from 70 to 90 fathoms [approximately 128 – 165m]. It then snapped like glass. The vessel then drifted nearly clear, stern foremost, but she lost her way – her sails filled, and she fell off before the wind and went right into the little bay', according to Robert Davison. Then the other anchor chain 'snapped like a carrot'. The *Tayleur* had been turning as if to sail clear of the cliffs, when a huge gust of wind filled the sails and pushed her back into harm's way. Now Captain Noble had no chance of directing the ship away from the rocks 'owing to the fury of the gale and high sea'. It seemed inevitable that the *Tayleur* would run aground.

A first class passenger and his friend made their way up top. 'On deck a horrible scene of confusion met my eye', he later told a newspaper. 'Before us at a short distance rose the bleak and rocky island, round the base of which the waves were dashing furiously while the vessel, quite unmanageable in the hands of her crew, drifted towards it with fearful rapidity'.

As a voice called "Breakers off the starboard bow!" the gale blew the *Tayleur* on at a sickening speed. As the tide ran into the bay, water rebounded from the near-vertical cliffs and cast the ship high on a back surge. The passengers on deck were screaming and drenched with spray, children were crying, and the ship creaked beneath them with the pressure of the waves. The captain and crew relayed orders as sails flapped and luggage shifted on the decks.

A desperate Captain Noble kept the sails braced full rather than ordering them hacked down with knives and hatchets. He was deliberately trying to swing the ship in broadside to the rocks, to give the passengers a chance of escape. This was an odd decision to make. The *Tayleur* had five sealed compartments in her hull; these were supposed to keep her afloat by preventing the ship from filling with water if the hull was breached; isolating the leak and allowing the vessel to remain buoyant. By aiming the *Tayleur* at the rocks in such a way as to have her impact on the jagged rocks side-on, Noble was making it all the more likely that several of the compartments would rupture, sinking the ship. In light of Noble's exhausted state, and the difficulty of responding rapidly to a crisis situation, this decision was understandable but still strange.

Hanging from the sides of the ship were seven lifeboats. A small steamboat was also tethered to the deck, intended for use on Australian rivers. There were nowhere near enough lifeboats to accommodate the approximately 650 people on board, but those eight vessels might have saved a few hundred, if they had been lowered before collision. But, as Noble later recalled, despite the pleas of passengers and some of the crew 'We made no attempt to lower the boats; they would not be able to live in the sea'.

Twenty-four-year-old William Jones was on deck, transfixed by the calamity unfolding before his eyes: 'The people [kept calling] out to the captain to lower the boats, but he said "What use?" and accordingly no boats were lowered; and the crew, as well as all the rest of the people, appeared utterly paralysed, and unable to do anything to save life'. It was far too crowded for Jones to see that, although there were pockets of paralysis amongst the hundreds gathered on deck, there was also a frenzy of activity elsewhere, as people fought to get to their loved ones and valuables.

Passengers and stewards who were not prostrate with seasickness below deck clattered up the steps in their hobnailed boots, some in just their nightgowns and bare feet, wailing and calling on God to deliver them safely from harm. With the women in his care now on deck, William Thompson left the poop cabin and joined them in the open:

I stood near the wheel, and to my horror, found we were rapidly approaching the rocks, which were only a few yards distant; in fact we were nearly alongside of them. I continued near the wheel, and while there the vessel struck with a terrible shock.

The rudder had evidently come into violent contact with the ground, and the afterpart of the ship was shaken, of which I had an unmistakable indication from the springing up of a portion of the deck under my feet. At this time the scene was one of a most appalling description. People ran wildly to and fro on the deck uttering the most piercing cries of distress, some called loudly for help, while others appeared quite paralysed and incapable of making any exertions to save themselves. The rock against which we were driven was precipitous, and the means of escape appeared almost cut off.

The *Illustrated London News* later reported: 'It was then blowing heavily, and a high sea running. It was then impossible to see a cable's length from the vessel, and in about twenty minutes more she struck with great violence on a reef of rocks running out from a creek right to the eastward bluff. The shock was tremendous, shaking the vessel from stem to stern. She rose on the next wave, and drove in rather broadside on; and when she struck again still heaving, the sea made a clean breach over her amidships [midsection], setting everything on deck afloat. After two or three more shocks, the ship began to sink by the stern, and the scene of confusion and dismay that ensued baffles all description; the passengers rushing up the hatchway, husbands carrying their children, and women lying prostrate on the deck with their infants, screaming and imploring help'.

None was forthcoming. The few people on the mainland who saw the *Tayleur* come to grief were dismissed as confused when they reported the wreck, their descriptions assumed to be about the wrecking of the *Scotland* the day before. The women cried out in vain.

Chapter Eight

And now began a scene of the most frightful horror – some running below to get what they could, others praying, some taking leave of their friends, wringing their hands, and beseeching them for help. The vessel, after striking, lay so close upon the rocks that several persons attempted to jump ashore. The first person who jumped struck his head against the rocks, and fell back into the water with his head frightfully cut, and, after struggling for a short time, sank. The next person who jumped from the vessel made good his footing, and was followed by several others – I believe belonging to the crew. They also succeeded in making good their landing and as soon as they had done so, scampered with all haste up the rocks, never attempting to assist those on board.

Several now swung themselves on the rocks, which were but a few feet from us. I managed to swing myself on shore, and retained the rope in my hand; I passed the end of it up to some of those behind, and by this means a great many were enabled to come on shore. To attempt to paint the heartrending scene on board the ship would be impossible – wives clinging to their husbands – children to their parents – women running wildly about the deck, uttering the most heartrending cries – many offering all they possessed to persons to get them on shore.

(A cabin passenger – probably William Jones,
Bury and Norwich Post, 1 February 1854)

**Saturday 21 January 1854,
Dublin Bay**

William Jones, a first class passenger from London, was lucky to reach the rocks with his life. While other first class passengers hid from the elements in their cabins, he had followed a group of women on deck. An enormous wave broke over the side of the slanting ship, washing away passengers, spars, boxes and the cabin where the first class passengers clustered together in terror. Those inside were either drowned or crushed to death.

Though he considered his fellow passengers 'a rascally lot', 21-year-old John Ryder was able to acknowledge the bravery he saw during the disaster. He had watched the first man attempt to escape the vessel, describing the rocks as having 'dashed' in the front of his head, yet he was impressed by the perseverance of others, as they attempted to rescue those still trapped on the ship. He explained:

A rope and a spar were afterwards got across, and by this means a number of lives were rescued, chiefly through the activity and devoted gallantry of one or two young men, passengers, whose exertions in saving the lives of their fellow-sufferers deserve the highest praise. Those who attempted to escape by the bows of the vessel, all, or nearly, met a miserable fate. The moment they fell into the water the waves caught them and dashed them violently against the rocks, and the survivors on shore could perceive the unfortunate creatures, with their heads bruised and cut open, struggling amidst the waves, and one by one sinking under them.

There was no beach or shore at the base of the cliffs. The water lay many fathoms deep, with just a rocky niche for survivors to aim for, amidst the crashing waves and swirling froth of the January sea. A Welsh miner, George Lewis, made it to the ledge with the end of a rope in his grasp. Somehow he fastened it amongst the protuberances of rock and helped 15 people to safety, risking his own life every time he took a hand from the craggy cliff face to pull them from the sea. Lewis fell into the water, overbalancing as he yanked a man from the surge of the waves, but managed to regain his position on the ledge without losing his hold on the lucky survivor.

Another first class passenger, George Cutts, who was emigrating with his wife Patty, was thinking of home when he remarked that the rock the *Tayleur* was impaled upon seemed 'higher than East Retford church steeple'. The *Tayleur* was an enormous ship, but the rough stone jutting out of the Irish Sea dwarfed even her highest masts. Captain Noble, his worst fears realised, called through a speaking trumpet to the passengers "You had better stick to the ship!" But the terrible noise of the sails flapping, the raw metal on the side of the ship grating against the rock, and the water pouring through the open hatches into the berths below to drown those frantically gathering together a few possessions, bundling their babies in shawls, or lying prone with seasickness in their beds, meant that few could hear him.

At this point John Ryder threw off his coat, and did his best to remain calm for 'all depended on it':

Richard [his friend] and I got down to the main chains; he took the end of a rope and swung ashore. I took another, but could not land for nearly five minutes. Directly the sea broke I jumped, and landed safely. Poor Horrell [a fellow passenger who had dashed below deck to alert Ryder of the danger they were in] lashed his nephew to his waist; I think I saw them among the dead. A rope was got from the ship, and several went ashore by that means; there were about ten souls on it when it snapped, and all were launched into eternity.

They then got a spar across; by it John Barfitt got ashore; several crowded on the spar, when it also broke, and another awful scene occurred. Our party, from first to last, stuck together, and of the 15 who lodged at Glover's, at Liverpool, all were saved but Horrell and his nephew. Many were saved, although not one out of three who made the attempt reached the land, most of them dropping into the sea, and of these there were only three or four who were saved. I jumped from the main channel (after great difficulty in getting there) on a rock, on which I had seen many perish in the leap.

Chivalrous first class passenger William Jones was still trapped on the wet, tilting deck:

The people crowded together to the head of the vessel, which was high out of the water when the stern went down; but the waves continued to wash over them, and each wave carried away some of the unfortunate passengers. The sea was so boisterous among the rocks that [I don't] think any of those who fell in the water were saved. All the weak and helpless were lost, and nobody who was not able to make an effort for himself was saved.

One woman on deck pleaded for help, crying, "I have £3,000 in my stays and I will give any man £200 who will take me on shore". Edward Tew Junior, a young bank clerk from Yorkshire, agreed to help. She promised him the whole £3,000 if he could just get her safely to shore, but then rushed off in a panic and when Tew tried to find her, she had vanished.

The sea was so rough, forcing the broken wood and bodies from the deck against the jagged black rocks, that any vessel lowered into the maelstrom had no chance of reaching the nearby cliff intact. But the passengers were frightened and panicking, and they sent a boat down anyway. It was immediately dashed to splinters in the frothing surge of tidal waters, and added to the debris sloshing about in the water between the people still aboard and the slimy rock that represented comparative safety.

Some of those on deck lashed together a makeshift raft and set it in the turbulent waters below the overhanging side of the ship. Dr Cunningham was trying desperately to calm the passengers on deck and move them away from the *Tayleur*'s one wooden mast, which the captain wanted to cut down with a hatchet to use as a bridge to the shore. Cunningham called out "Who will take my wife on shore and I will give him any money?" James McLellan, one of the crew, replied "Hand your lady to me and I'll try". As McLellan later recalled, 'he did hand her and I was carrying her off to a raft that was floating and we could have made the land I am sure but the passengers rushed upon me and I was obliged to let her go to save myself. Oh it was a dreadful sight'.

Among the first to safely reach the shore was the assistant cook. He fixed a rope to the rocks, the wet hemp rough in his hands, as half a dozen other crewmen joined him. They rigged up a spar as a bridge and helped some of the passengers over it, as the assistant cook scrambled across the slippery rocks to the cliff towering above them. Eager to throw more lengths of the pale hemp down to the lucky few on the rocks below, some shoved at the hapless passengers and crew struggling to remain upright on a deck littered with coils of rope. Once the rope was made fast to the masts or the sides of the ship, those left behind hoped to climb to safety. But this would only be possible if they kept hold of the rope.

James Oldfield, a steerage passenger, clambered to safety using the spar. Looking back, he surveyed the scene: 'Numbers were stationed at the side of the vessel waiting for a chance to lay hold on the ropes which had been flung out – though many of those who did succeed in that object only the sooner met their deaths. It was one of the most agonising sights ever witnessed by mortal eye to see so many human beings especially women and children doomed to destruction almost within grasp of shore'.

As Captain Noble later said, "If the passengers had kept clear until the foremast was cut away I have no doubt on my mind but that nine tenths of them would have been saved. From the manner in which they were crowding about and the confusion, if I cut it away, it would have killed more than were drowned". They were so close to safety.

Brave Liverpudlian William Thompson observed that:

The starboard side of the vessel was alongside the rocks and she was distant at one end about thirty or forty feet but much nearer at the other. In fact, it appeared possible by a great effort, to leap from the fore part of the ship to the rock; and several of the more active and expert among the passengers though at a considerable risk, took this opportunity of jumping on shore. Some of them I believe fell into the sea, and were drowned in making the attempt.

At this time the deck was as may naturally be imagined, a scene of the most indescribable confusion, and little could be done by the captain, his officers and crew, in endeavouring to save the lives of the unfortunate people whose destruction appeared inevitable. With considerable difficulty a rope was passed from the ship and made fast on the rock by those who had in the first instance been so fortunate as to gain access to it. I told all who inquired of me to avail themselves of the rope as the only probable means of escape and to do so as quickly as possible.

Some did so, sliding down to the rock, but as Thompson witnessed, this grew more difficult as the ship moved, gradually rolling over towards the sea.

After a number of people had passed down the rope to the rock, I decided upon adopting this method of escape. I took a rope's end in my left hand to increase the means of escape and, placing myself on the rope which formed this communication between the ship and the rock, slid down and reached the land in safety.

The women were afraid to venture down the ropes which in the earlier part of the calamity would not have been very difficult. When the vessel struck there was a heavy sea running and from the height of the rocks and the difficulty of access to it, little chance existed of persons saving their lives by swimming. Several made the attempt, but few if any succeeded; they were swept away by the surf and many who clung to spars and other portions of the ship shared the same fate.

… During the confusion which took place on deck the Captain ordered the steward to go to the cabins and let no one in. The steward obeyed his orders, went to the cabin, and is supposed to have perished there for shortly afterwards two heavy seas [waves], one immediately following the other, swept the deck and carried away the poop cabin and its contents. A fine young man named Wilson, from Glasgow, was observed to go into the cabin, and he was not seen afterwards; he was amongst those who perished.

Thompson could only watch as the ship rolled, settling into deeper water. He saw those still on deck gather 'about the bowsprit and the fore part of the ship, this being the only portion that remained afloat. Very few were saved'. Though most of the passengers and crew assumed it either useless or too dangerous to try escaping from the furthermost side of the ship, one second class passenger thought differently. Twenty-six-year-old Edward Tew Junior came from a comfortable life in Yorkshire. He was an educated and intelligent young man, born to a Justice of the Peace and raised in Crofton Hall, next door to the school the Brontë sisters had attended. Nothing could have prepared him for the wrecking of the *Tayleur*, but he rose to the occasion and helped where he could.

I [was] actively engaged from the time we first saw land. I had no time to be frightened. I was one of the few who kept their senses to the last. I went to the larboard side of the vessel – that is to say the side furthest from the shore. I sat down for about half a minute and made up my mind to swim in rather a different direction, in order to avoid the dead bodies. I then dropped quietly down a chain into the water, and had not swum above a couple of yards when I saw a boy, about ten years old, clinging to a piece of wood.

Immediately I made to him; he was crying and told me his mother was drowned. He said it was no use my trying to save him, for he should be drowned. However, I was determined to try, and accordingly took him by the collar and placed him on the top of a large spar, and made him take hold of a piece of iron which was standing out. I still held his collar with my right hand, and kept the broken pieces of wood and spars off with my left hand. It was then that I experienced difficulties which required a most superhuman effort to overcome.

A heavy sea was rolling over us every moment, large spars threatening to crush us, and almost perpendicular rocks, as black as death, staring us in the face. I was determined not to have our heads dashed against the rocks, as had been the fate of so many of my fellow passengers. As we neared the rocks, the boy was washed off the spar, but I still had hold of him. I put out my hand to save our heads, and received a cut in the hand, but I felt the land and told the boy we were saved. But not so, for we were washed back again. I made to land a second time, and was washed back again.

I tried a third time, and was treated the same way. I was making toward the rock a fourth time, determined to save the lad or die with him, when a spar struck him on the right side of his head – the side I had no control over – and entered his skull. It knocked me under at the same time, but I rose again, and a rope was thrown to me, which I twisted round my arm 20 times at least, and with the assistance of a sailor clambered up the rock.

Meanwhile the assistant cook, (records are uncertain but probably 31-year-old Seymour Prard from Bombay), was climbing the near-vertical cliff. Its steepness was obscured by thick grey fog, so the survivors could not see its full height. The wind buffeted him and the screams from those still on board the *Tayleur* would have accompanied him as he rose into the fog and lost sight of the shipwreck. Eventually he made it to the grass-covered rock near the top. Taking care not to slip on tufts slick with rain, he climbed higher, then eased himself over the edge and into the field above the stormy bay. He was completely alone.

Chapter Nine

The scene was now most truly awful. The most desperate struggles for life were made by the wretched passengers – great numbers of women jumped overboard in the vain hope of reaching land, and the ropes were crowded by hundreds who, in their eagerness, terror, and confusion, frustrated each other's efforts for self-preservation. Many of the females would get half-way and then become unable to proceed further; and, after clinging to the rope for a short time, would be forced from their hold by those who came after them …

Two men came on shore with children tied to their backs. … I saw one fine girl, who, after falling from the rope, managed to get hold of another one, which was hanging from the side of the ship, and which she held on to for more than a quarter of an hour, the sea every moment dashing her against the side of the ship, but it was impossible for us to lend her any assistance. Someone got a spar out, by which several got on shore; but it soon broke, and now might be seen hundreds hanging to the bulwarks of the ship, each struggling to get on shore. I saw one young woman hanging on the middle of the rope for some time by her two hands, but those pushing to get on shore soon sent her to her doom.

(Mr W. Jones, 'an intelligent gentleman from London', *Tayleur* cabin passenger, *Leeds Times*, 28 January 1854)

**Saturday 21 January 1854,
Dublin Bay**

The passengers and crew were in a cold, wet hell. Those still standing on the deck were soaked from the water sloshing over the floor and the rain. Layers of coarse fabric and starched linen would have clung to their skin and dragged heavily on their bodies, leeching their strength and making it harder to move. William Thompson, now on the rocks, called to them to throw down more ropes. If those on board could not use them to descend, then the men on the rocks might toss them into the water to aid the people struggling there. When his shouts went unheard due to 'the confusion which prevailed and the roaring of the surf', he tried holding out his hands to those carried along by the tide. Yet 'owing to the rise and fall of the waves we did not succeed, and many of the poor struggling creatures perished within our sight'.

Amongst the hundreds still clinging to life in the bay, Dr Cunningham and his family were highly noticeable. The ship was rocking under their feet, its great metal bulk tipping at an increasingly precarious angle. If he was going to save his family, it was now or never. Clasping baby George tight to his chest, Cunningham used his other hand to follow the rope over the side. With the little boy's clothing clenched between his teeth, the surgeon inched his way along the slippery spar wedged against the side of the ship. Moving carefully towards the safety of the rock, battered all the while by spray, they almost made it. The doctor 'had succeeded in getting about halfway to the shore', according to W. Jones of London, but then:

> the ship lurched outwards, by which the rope was dragged from the hands of those who held it on the lower rocks, and was held only by those above, thus running him high in the air, so that the brave fellow could not drop on the rock. Word was now given to lower the rope gently; but those who held it above let it go by the run, and the poor fellow, with his child, was buried in the waves; but in a short time he again appeared above the water, manfully battling with the waves and the portions of the wreck that now floated about him. He at length swam to a ladder hanging by a rope alongside the ship, and got upon it.

George had joined the other children drowned between the ship and the rocks. But Cunningham still had his wife Susan and their elder son Henry to save. Captain Noble helped to strap the anxious four-year-old to his father's back, then the young doctor tried again. As a private letter from an unnamed *Tayleur* survivor to Cunningham's family in Fife later revealed, somehow this son was lost to the stormy waters too. Cunningham could have saved himself, but at that point chose to go back for Susan instead. As the letter explained: 'His wife, who had undergone the anguish of witnessing in succession the destruction of her children, and the fearful danger of her husband, was now on her knees on the deck, apparently in a state of fearful distraction. Her husband endeavoured to rouse her, parted her hair from her face, and fastened it in a knot behind, and then led her over the side of the vessel, and for the third time, heavily burdened, attempted to gain the shore'.

Many of the survivors noted the Scotsman's courage and cool-headedness, and his tender demeanour towards his wife. Half-carrying her in his arms, he helped her along one of the poles, holding tight to the rope once again. He urged her on, refusing to give up despite the loss of their children. 'He had reached the rocks, and was almost safe, when a heavy surge carried both into the water. Cunningham, still retaining hold of his wife, again succeeded in catching hold of a rope hanging from the ship's side. He caused her likewise to take hold of the rope, and they held themselves thus suspended for some considerable time. At length Mrs Cunningham dropped from her hold, while he at the same time grasped her; both went down'.

Susan was apparently swept under the vessel by the undertow. According to the *Manchester Times*, Dr Cunningham could still have saved himself 'but seeing a poor woman in the act of sinking, he swam over to her assistance, when she, with the energy of despair, seized hold of him in such a manner as to render his struggles to swim unavailing, and they both sank together'. The woman panicked and tried to climb on him, holding the brave doctor under until he couldn't help but breathe in salt water. The sea would have burned in his nose and throat, stinging his eyes, as Cunningham thrashed his limbs in a vain attempt to break free. His final breath bubbled to the surface as his body sank under the water. With the doctor's death, the woman was also lost.

As the ship moved against the rock, drowning those still inside and releasing great belches of trapped air and crushed bodies from the wreck, other attempts at rescue also fell foul of the tidal surge. Rebecca Chasey, a 28-year-old dressmaker from Bristol, was travelling with her husband and baby to the Australian goldfields. She had worked as a nursemaid for the Folwell family, who ran a successful hackney-cab business, and the Folwells' adult son, Edward, was also on board the *Tayleur*. Rebecca had been lying in her berth with the baby when they hit the rocks, and raced on deck with her husband and son, clad in just her loose white gown and nightcap.

Edward Folwell told the *Devizes and Wiltshire Gazette* of their ordeal later:

The ship rolled dreadfully and the scene of terror and confusion on deck was of the most agonising character. Some seized spars or pieces of the deck furniture and threw themselves overboard, in the hope of drifting onto the rock, but the commotion of the sea was too violent and they were for the most part either drowned or beaten against the rocks and killed. A large number of the crew were the first to get on shore; they ran nimbly up the rocks, and sat looking on without, as far as I could see, rendering any assistance…

During the short interval of the striking of the ship and my getting on to the rock, I saw many heart-rending sights. I witnessed the death of poor Chasey's husband and child. The poor fellow, with a manly devotion, insisted on his wife, who had just come from her berth, being got on shore first, and strapped his infant to his back for the purpose of following her. She was lowered down a rope into the water, and was hauled onto the shore by two or three men. He then got on to the line, and was descending it when the vessel gave a roll, the rope broke, and he and his child perished in the surge.

The paper commented on Rebecca's behalf, perhaps because to quote her directly like the men would have been thought unseemly:

To make the descent from the ship, which was rolling and pitching under the influence of the breakers, was a work, she describes, of great difficulty, and she is almost induced to wonder how she could have mustered strength enough to accomplish it … When she effected her escape, she had nothing on but her frock and bonnet, and everything of which she and her husband were possessed went down with the ship, leaving her, not only childless and a widow, but in a strange place without a penny in her possession.

But the rocks were by no means a safe place. The Millers (an Irish family not to be confused with another Miller family on board the ship) were rescued by their son, Hugh, who was a powerful swimmer. He managed to get them on to the rocks, only for the waves to wash them off one at a time. Hugh grew tired and sank, leaving only his younger brother James alive. Those on the rocks knew the dangers, and the cliffs loomed over them with the promise of escape, but for some the temptation to help those just a few feet away was too great to resist. The screams and wails, then sudden silences, of the drowning passengers and crew were still audible to those reaching for them and urging them on.

The ship rolled away from the land 10 or 20 minutes after she hit the rocks, tilting her deck at a precarious angle and jolting many of those left on deck into the rough white froth of sea and wreckage. It broke the ropes, and also knocked makeshift bridges loose, leaving enormous splintery lengths of wood adrift in the water. Passenger James Oldfield noticed one woman hauling herself onto a plank, clinging to it for some time as efforts were made to save her, all in vain.

The Carby family were then on deck, shaking with cold. Samuel was a seasoned sailor after his long voyage to the Antipodes and back, but his wife and son were unaccustomed to life at sea and terribly seasick. Sarah and Robert had been lying in their berth in just their night clothes, feeling wretched, when Samuel raced down the stairs to fetch them. Water was already coursing into the passengers' quarters through the hatches as he grabbed them by the hands and dragged them barefoot up on deck. Their fortune of 200 gold sovereigns, stitched securely into Sarah's corsets, now lay abandoned in her berth. They had been in too much of a hurry to grab it, and the weight would have slowed them down anyway. Too many of their fellow passengers had fallen from the ropes already, laden with saturated clothes and secret treasures. Samuel urged Robert over the side and onto the rocks, where the 13-year-old waited anxiously for his mother. Like Rebecca Chasey, Sarah's loose nightshirt helped her greatly. Other women were burdened with a dozen layers of restrictive clothing, all now sodden and impossible to strip off quickly. The ropes were crowded with people waiting for the next person to fall into the water beneath, so they could inch closer to the wet black rocks just a few feet away.

As the *Stamford Mercury* reported:

in their eagerness, terror, and confusion, [they] frustrated each other's efforts
for self-preservation. Many of the females proceeded half way, and then
became unable to go forward, and after clinging to the rope for a short time
were forced from their hold by those who followed. Mrs Carby had got part
of the way across when her legs fell, and she hung some time by her two
hands over the raging sea: her husband then went on the rope, and managed
to assist her to the rock.

Along with Ann Carty, Rebecca Chasey and Sarah Carby were the only
three of over a hundred women passengers to survive the calamity. Although
the *Birkenhead* disaster two years before had set a standard of women and
children being rescued first in times of great danger, this didn't happen on
the frenzied top deck of the *Tayleur*.

HM Steamer *Birkenhead* had been carrying a mixture of troops and their
families when it wrecked on South Africa's Danger Point reef. The men
stood to attention on deck while the lifeboats got to safety, then those who
had not already drowned in their bunks attempted to swim the two miles
to shore. Newspapers of the time reported that the compass gave a false
reading due to the steamer's iron hull, leading the ship astray in the early
morning darkness. Of the approximately 643 people aboard, 193 survived,
including all the women and children. The surviving soldiers only left the
ship as the deck sank beneath the water, clinging to pieces of wreckage.
'[M]any of them, whilst struggling in the angry element, were seized by
sharks, their yells being heard by many of those who so miraculously escaped
a similar fate', (*Herts Guardian*, 1852).

There were no man-eating sharks to worry about in the area of the Irish
Sea where the *Tayleur* wrecked, but the situation was no less lethal. Many
families perished together, the men refusing to leave their children as
they sank under the waves; drowning with them, though they could have
abandoned their offspring and reached land. However, there was no general
move to save the women and children before the men sought safety beneath
the cliffs. Unlike the *Birkenhead*, the *Tayleur* was not a ship of disciplined
soldiers, and chaos prevailed in the storm. Not one survivor of the ragged
mass who finally mustered at the top of the cliffs later remembered hearing
an order to evacuate or even to raise the alarm below decks. The onus was on

individuals to save families, friends, and bunkmates: it was up to them to do what they felt to be the right thing.

Thomas Kemp, a passenger in first class, later recollected to the *Manchester Times*:

I was all this time on the ship endeavouring to facilitate the escape of my friends; but I now saw escape, at least for the females, was absolutely impossible. Just at that instant a rope was made fast to the spritsail-yard end, and as the ship was leaning over very considerably from shore, I had great difficulty in crawling up to that point where the rope was fastened; and when I was nearly at this point the rope broke, but providentially a small line was attached to the other end, and (thanks be to the Almighty) by that means I was able to effect my escape. At this period the vessel was sinking very fast, the sea making a clean breach over her.

Previously the scene had been most distressing, but now it was harrowing in the extreme, for by every succeeding wave 1, 2, 10, 20, or 50 were washed off; and such was the position of the vessel, so rugged were the rocks, and the surge was so violent, that to escape alive from the water was almost miraculous, and it was impossible to render any assistance.

As the paper relayed to its horrified readers, Kemp 'had a hairbreadth escape': 'He was swinging himself on shore by the rope suspended from the bowsprit, when he missed his footing and fell into the water whence he was rescued by a man on the rock, who succeeded in catching hold of his trousers as he was about to sink'. Kemp's pragmatic attitude in abandoning the women, and a lucky grab from a stranger, had saved him.

American passenger Patrick O'Higgins testily commented in the *Dundee, Perth, and Cupar Advertiser*: 'I have no doubt that a large number of the females could have been saved only for their own obstinacy in clinging to the masts and refusing to be slung on shore. I had a rope round the waists of two of them, and was going to throw them on to the rocks, when I saw some men dashed to pieces, and I got alarmed'.

The water was not just thick with froth and fallen bodies, it was also full of wood and luggage washed over from the deck. The violence with which the water slammed the items against the passengers and crew in the water, and hurled them against the jagged rocks, stripped the unluckiest of their clothes and dismembered them before the eyes of their fellow travellers. Drowned babies bobbed in the water. People watched their friends float by with torn limbs, battered faces and the vacant expression of the dead. Heads surfaced through the froth, bodies swayed below; petticoats bloomed pale in the depths.

Whole groups were lost to the tidal swell, including all ten members of the Boar family, and a party of five sisters. A seaman travelling in the intermediate quarters of the ship had been engaged in 'taking some money from his chest, when a lame girl frantic[al]ly appealed to him to save her. He left his chest, but when he reached the deck he was compelled to abandon her, and barely succeeded in saving himself, having lost all he was worth'. The girl was one of a group of five sisters, none of whom survived the wrecking according to the *Dundee, Perth, and Cupar Advertiser*.

Samuel Brockman of Falkirk had been one of the first to make it safely to the rocks. He told the *Glasgow Herald*:

> *There were only about a dozen before me. One-half of these took to the hill, without as much as looking back to their perishing companions. When I looked at the sinking vessel I saw my sister (Mrs McPherson) and her husband with their little girl, three-years-old, sitting between them. The sea was running very high. A wave came and washed my sister overboard; while I was watching her to see if I could save her the child went over too – at least next moment I saw her in the water. McPherson was washed out and in the vessel's bulwarks several times before he let go. [He] had a life buoy attached to his person; but it was too low down, and in consequence of that he never got his head out of the water, and so he was drowned. His wife was seen floating for some time, and the child at some distance from her; but no assistance could be rendered her, and she perished along with little Agnes.*

There were no such things as safety drills for passengers in those days, nor were life-jackets or buoys supplied for every person on board. *The Life-boat* commented in 1857 on how 'imperfectly informed, how supinely indifferent, is the great bulk of our population as to the causes, the prevention, or the mitigation of the horrors of shipwreck!'. 'The fact that emigrant and other passenger vessels do not carry a sufficient number of available boats to carry all on board them is so generally known that we need hardly repeat it'. Despite there being at least 1,115 vessels wrecked in the waters around Great Britain and Ireland in a 12 month period just two years before, there was still no move to improve these woefully inadequate measures. This type of equipment was deemed impractical, and even unsafe, with concerns raised about how little room there would be on deck if the amount of equipment stored there was increased.

Apart from Ellen Rimes, a four-year-old who made it to land strapped to her father, her mother Betsey lost in the wreck, and Robert Bunning, only one other minor out of 70 is known to have survived. An elderly emigrant (thought to be German or possibly French) was preparing to climb overboard after a heavy wave had sluiced even the steamboat secured to the top deck from the wreck of the ship. He cast a final glance over his shoulder and spied a baby lying alone in the water on deck. Perhaps the child's clothing had air trapped inside it, or maybe it held its breath when the swell broke over the ship. Just as the unlucky Dr Cunningham had done only a few minutes before, the old man clamped the baby's dress in his teeth and made for the rocks. One other infant was reported to have been washed onto the rocks or carried there on a man's back, but its fate remains a mystery. Battered against the rocks, his body bruised and one arm broken, the elderly German clambered up the rock to safety still clutching the shivering child. Others took the burden from him, some hoping to identify it as their own lost child.

Captain Noble could only stand by and watch as the passengers and crew he had hoped to transport round the world drowned before his eyes. As massive waves engulfed his ship, only the ropes wrapped round his body kept the captain from being washed off the deck. Noble and the second mate, Edward Kewley, waited until the last possible minute before abandoning the *Tayleur*. The captain stripped off his blue frock coat and outer layers of clothing until he stood waist-deep in water wearing just his trousers and a flannel shirt. Jumping into the crashing sea, they swam for the shore, avoiding the larger pieces of wreckage as best they could. Kewley was overwhelmed by the waves and drowned, but Noble reached the water near the rocks exhausted and covered in terrible cuts and bruises. Two young men reached down to grasp his arms and haul him to safety, but as Noble grabbed onto the rock the next wave washed away his saviours. He spoke later of how his feet had accidentally touched their dead bodies in the water.

In the meantime, the ship's cook and a few others had run off to find help. David Pratt of Dundee, second purser on the *Tayleur*, later recounted his ordeal to the *Dundee, Perth, and Cupar Advertiser*. He had been in a fortunate position when the ship struck:

> *so close and steep, too, were the rocks at this point that I stepped from the main chains to the shore, the guard-board of the chains being only some three or four feet above the rock. A Chinaman was the first to land, and after getting up towards the cliff looked down complacently upon the hundreds who were by this time fast being swept away and swallowed in the waves.*
>
> *As soon as I got ashore I sung out to throw a rope to me, to which a hawser [thick rope or cable used for mooring a ship] should be tied, so that I might secure it to the rock, and thus enable numbers to get ashore in the event of the ship surging off or sinking in deep water. Someone threw me a rope, but as it was part of the running rigging, I desired them to cut it and tie a hawser to the end, so that I might haul it ashore; but this was not done, although I bawled myself hoarse ... the vessel began to settle by the stern, and the sea made a complete breach over [the deck at that end], and the passengers at once rushed forward to endeavour to get ashore by two spars which extended about 20 feet from the fore part of the ship to the rocks. I stood with the line in my hands for more than ten minutes, calling in vain for a hawser to be attached to it, until I was at last obliged to leave the rock, in consequence of the sea rising and washing over me ... in about a quarter of an hour after the ship struck, finding I could get no one to throw a warp [tow-rope] or hawser, and being all but swept away by the waves, I left the rock, and scrambling up the cliff went in search of assistance. After walking some distance I came across a small cabin, and the people there directed me to a coast guard station about half a mile further on.*

In the space of less than an hour, just two days after leaving Liverpool, over half of the people who had boarded the *Tayleur* were dead.

THE POOR MAN'S FRIEND.

'The Poor Man's Friend' (John Leech, *Punch*, 1845): 'Death is the poor man's doctor' is an old Irish (and German) saying. For many of those struggling to make ends meet during the nineteenth century, Death was also their friend.

(*Right*) Diggers in Australia, looking for the glint of gold that could mean riches. No sign of the clouds of maggot-bearing blowflies awaiting fresh immigrants are apparent in this cheery advert. (All images are from the *Illustrated London News*, 21 August 1852)

(*Left*) Men with cabbage-leaf hats working the riverbed in hopes of finding grains washed downstream. Pictures like this helped would-be emigrants to make their decision, and showed them what to do once out there.

(*Right*) Children were set to work 'cradling' for gold, rocking the contraption using a handle to encourage dirt to wash through the sieve whilst retaining any gold for collection. Tedious work, but safer than being stuck up a chimney or dodging lethal machinery in a mill.

Dry-digging for gold and quartz deposits with not a hard hat in sight and just a tree trunk encouraging the roof to stay up. This was dangerous and exhausting work, but it could make them a fortune. (*Illustrated London News,* 21 August 1852)

Gold-diggers resting amongst tents and camp fires. An idyllic scene of relaxation and enjoyment after a hard day's work, with their tools shown prominently in the foreground. (*Illustrated London News,* 29 May 1852)

(*Below*) Emigration agent's office – with their passage money paid, there was little for emigrants to do but wait until their berths became available. (*Illustrated London News,* 10 May 1851)

(*Left*) An advert for one of *Tayleur*'s earlier departure dates in the *Freeman's Journal* including glowing praise for Captain Noble. The ship sailed three months later than planned. (© *The British Library Board. All Rights Reserved. Image reproduced with kind permission of The British Newspaper Archive www.britishnewspaperarchive.co.uk*)

(*Above*) A contemporary artist's impression of RMS *Tayleur* sailing with the White Star Line pennant flying high. (*Illustrated London News,* 26 November 1853)

Images of emigrants from the *Illustrated London News*, 6 July 1850: (*Left*) Hubbub of travellers around the Government Medical Inspectors' office near the docks. (*Below*) Passengers waiting to board, guarding their luggage. (*Bottom*) Emigrants departing for Australia, luggage at their feet and hats in the air. Many would never see their homeland again.

Images of emigrants from the *Illustrated London News*, 6 July 1850: (*Above*) Roll call on the deck of an emigrant ship. A crewman checks the names of those on board. A lifeboat hangs on davits to the side. (*Middle*) Men with lanterns and an illicit candle check amongst the luggage for stowaways. Five were found on the *Tayleur*. (*Below*) Even in the cramped, chaotic passengers' quarters below decks, the men wore top hats.

(*Above*) Hat boxes, baskets and bags are tied near their owners' berths, while on the right a tea set is laid out (*ILN*, 10 May 1851). (*Middle*) A child watches from an upper berth as people dance to a fiddler's tune in the passengers' quarters (*ILN*, 6 July 1850). (*Below*) An artist's impression of the ship wrecking against the rocks, the people on deck in touching distance of safety. The gap was larger in reality, and the sea more ferocious. (*ILN, 28 January 1854*)

(*Above*) View of the wreck site from the top of Lambay's cliffs. The small boat is tethered above what remains of the Tayleur. (*With kind permission of Eoghan Kieran*)

(*Below*) Noble's gravestone in Liverpool. A large stone, with room for the details of a whole family or messages of respect and admiration from his peers, it provides minimal information. (*Photograph by Gill Hoffs*)

IN MEMORY
of
CAPT JOHN NOBLE
WHO DEPARTED THIS LIFE JULY 24 1861,
AGED 35 YEARS

Chapter Ten

Of all the disasters recorded during a season unhappily distinguished by such calamities, not one has been announced of a character more truly horrifying than the dreadful shipwreck reported in our impression of yesterday. It is scarcely possible to exaggerate the terrors of so frightful a catastrophe. This very day last week the Tayleur, *a stately ship of more than 2,000 tons burden, carrying a valuable cargo, and freighted with nearly 600 emigrants, sailed from Liverpool for Australia with every conceivable prospect of a fortunate voyage.*

The vessel itself was of iron, perfectly new, and so splendidly constructed as to have been pronounced one of the most magnificent specimens afloat. She was commanded by a captain of "great experience and ability; the weather was fine, the wind fair, and, as she left the Mersey in tow of a steam-tug to commence her course, it seemed as if no ship had ever gone out of harbour with promise of a better run." In eight-and-forty short hours from that moment the Tayleur *was a perfect wreck, and out of her complement of 660 souls not 300 were left alive.*

(*Bury and Norwich Post*, 1 February 1854)

**Early afternoon, Saturday 21 January 1854,
Lambay**

A few survivors, among them David Pratt and the ship's cook, went in search of a coastguard, telling the few people they met of the terrible fate of the *Tayleur* nearby. The Dockrell family were eating a meal when a man wearing seafaring clothes burst into their cottage. He spoke 'a foreign language', but somehow managed to make himself understood and the Dockrells followed him back to the wreck site to help. Meanwhile, those still alive in the storm-tossed bay gazed at the cliffs looming over the stricken ship. The clifftops were shrouded in thick grey fog and only brief glimpses could be seen of their full height. Waves still swept the rocks while the rest of the survivors clung on. There were no signs of life nearby; as far as they knew, they were on their own.

As the ship tilted away from the rocks, casting towards the mountainous waves, two men decided against taking their chances in the water with the ropes and chains dangling from the crowded edges of the *Tayleur* and instead climbed higher up the rigging. As Captain Noble reached safety and the baby was carried onto the rocks, dangling from the mouth of its rescuer, the ship settled deeper into the water, until only her masts remained visible. The wind whipped the sails, howling through the rigging, which was held at an angle by masts pointing out to sea. One by one, those still pleading for help amid the wreckage sank into silence. Now only the sobs of survivors and cries for the lost could be heard, as they searched for friends and family members amongst the bedraggled scraps of humanity beneath the cliffs. Turning their backs on the water, where more than half the passengers floated between the poles and barrels, the surviving 280 people began to climb. The two men in the rigging beseeched them to help them to shore and not to leave them trapped there above the water, but to no avail. The sea was still too rough to risk a rescue attempt. About an hour after the *Tayleur* hit the rocks, the survivors gathered together. Shuddering with cold and shock in their ripped, sodden clothing and often bare feet, they decided to clamber upwards in search of help.

Following 'a very rugged and dangerous path', as survivor Thomas Kemp later described it to the *Stamford Mercury*, the shivering masses dragged themselves over the rocks, cutting their feet to shreds as they climbed to the slippery grass above. John Nicholls, unable to put any weight on his damaged foot, was carried by some of the more able men as others nursed broken arms and battered heads. 'Of those whose lives had been saved many were shockingly maimed, through having been beaten about in the surf and forced against the rocks', Edward Folwell told the *Bristol Mercury*. 'Some had their arms broken, some their ankles dislocated, and a man whom I saw get up the rocks after me had his nose nearly torn off and all his teeth knocked in'.

Noble, perhaps dazed from his ordeal in the water, asked the men near him for matches – which would have been sodden and useless in the wind and rain, even if dry firewood had been available. None had any, and his request stirred suspicions amongst the cannier seamen and passengers that their captain had no idea of their location. At least one of the passengers had known where they had landed, though. A bottle washed up on one of the Isles of Cumbrae just off the Ayrshire coast a few months later. It contained a hastily-pencilled note, which read 'On board the *Tayleur*, on striking Lambay Island. Many of the passengers and crew are now drowning before my eyes, and no assistance. My wife is also lost. William Clough, Manchester'. Clough did not make it onto the island alive.

A shepherd greeted the survivors as they moved away from the edge of the cliffs, before the gusting winds could blow them back over. The local coastguard was now on his way, as were the Dockrells and the foreign seaman. They arrived at the scene as the last of the straggling crowd prepared to leave the cliff top. Thomas Willet, a passenger who had previously been a porter at the Manchester Natural History Society Museum, beseeched the coastguard to save the two men still swaying in the rigging far below. But the coastguard pragmatically refused to risk the lifeboat in the treacherous waters at the bottom of the cliff.

The shepherd directed the group towards some of the cottages peppering the grassy island. Fewer than a hundred people lived there, mainly fishing and crofting families who scraped a living. There were no shops for the *Tayleur* survivors to try to barter clothes or provisions from. The islanders saved what little they could spare during the summer for the long lean months of winter, when they were sometimes cut off from the nearby Irish mainland for days at a time. Despite the scarcity of their supplies, they opened their houses, cupboards and barn to approximately 283 men, three women and a couple of children, welcoming them into the warm wherever they could fit them in.

Lambay's former name was *Reachra*, Gaelic for 'the place of many shipwrecks', due to its dangerous coast. As captains usually managed to steer a course around it, shipwrecks grew less common and the island had been renamed from the Old Norse *lamb-ey* (lamb island) for its use in grazing sheep. There were signs of human habitation on the island dating back several thousand years, including the remains of defences against Spanish pirates, and it was thought to have been the first part of Ireland invaded by Vikings. But now there were just some cottages, a coastguard station, and local nobleman Lord Talbot's castle, all of which were opened to the shivering survivors.

The anonymous baby boy 'was placed under the protection of a poor cottager, whose wife resolved to adopt it as her own', while John Nicholls – who was in a lot of pain with a dislocated foot – and the survivors with the worst injuries were gently loaded into a cart and removed to the castle. Lord Talbot's steward, Mr Cusack, allowed some of the men, including Jonathan Carter from Lancashire, to kill a fat pig and bring in potatoes from the store. He welcomed many in, particularly the most badly wounded and those of an obviously higher social class, and straw was strewn about the floors to give the freezing passengers and crew a warmer, more comfortable place to lie down and rest. Two giant coppers were set to boiling in the castle kitchen, one containing the whole carcass of the slaughtered pig, the other two potatoes each for the hungry survivors. Some were given oatmeal, too. It was a lot of food for the island community to give up, especially with several difficult months still ahead, but amongst so many it made little difference.

With the weather still raging any attempts the coastguard may have made at semaphore against the white wall of their station were rendered useless. Lambay was barely visible from Malahide just a couple of miles away, and there was no hope of further assistance reaching the island that afternoon.

The coastguards had not given up on the men stranded amongst the *Tayleur*'s sails, despite the towering waves and howling winds. 'All they could do was to attempt to save the two who were in the rigging', as William Jones, a passenger from London, later told the *Manchester Times*. 'They managed to get a line to one of them by fastening two lines, at the end of which was a piece of wood, to a single line, and guiding it from the rock to the spot where the poor fellow was, so that he could reach it. They then dragged him ashore. There was one fine young man left in the top, but they could not reach him, and when he saw them going away his cries were heartrending'.

Some of the stronger survivors assisted with salvage, pulling parcels, sea chests, boxes, casks and spars above the high-tide mark. Grabbing what they could, the men hauled the bulky objects to a dip in the field beside the coastguards' cottages. Trunks and luggage served as makeshift shelter for those unfortunate passengers and crew who had failed to gain accommodation for the night on the hay-strewn floors of the cottages, castle, or barn. As the tide started to go out, more of the wreckage washed ashore, leaving the islanders with plentiful supplies of firewood, rope, and timber. The receding water also left bodies in its wake. All the men could do at this point was pull them higher up the shore, and wait for morning.

The Carby family huddled together in one of the cottages, along with little Ellen Rimes and her father, and a few other survivors. Samuel Carby was no stranger to the cruel whims of fate and accustomed to making the best of unpleasant situations. The third of four illegitimate children born to Alice Carby in Lincolnshire during the early 1800s, he had started life on the lowest rung of the social ladder. But Samuel somehow learned how to read and write and became a brickmaker, having previously worked as an agricultural labourer round the fields of Stamford, Lincolnshire. Young seamstress Sarah Bunning had his baby, and by December 1841 she had moved in to his mother's house, while they prepared for their wedding.

One night that month Samuel and his friend, George Bell, a roguish sort, were drinking in their local pub, the White Swan. George was a couple of inches taller than Samuel, ruddy faced, with brown hair, scars, and his initials tattooed on the back of his left hand. He also had a partner called Sarah, a little boy, Henry, born out of wedlock and a habit of poaching. According to newspaper reports, on their way home, the pair wandered past a field full of sheep. George went over to one with the number 66 branded on its side, and drunkenly proceeded to slaughter it, hacking off a couple of chunks of fresh mutton with the wool still attached. The men squelched about in the mud for a bit, leaving clear tracks, before turning in for the night.

The next day, Sarah Bunning was making dinner when she noticed a lump of meat in the cupboard. Perhaps Samuel explained it away, perhaps he told her the truth. In any case they ate it, and Sarah thought nothing more of the matter – or so she later claimed – until she went out on the Monday and heard that a local farmer had reported one of his sheep missing. She raced home, and retrieved another hunk of mutton. Tucking it into her petticoats, Sarah set off down Wothorpe Road until she came to a hedgerow. After a quick glance to check that no one was watching, she bent down, fished the meat out from beneath her skirts, and threw it over the hedge. But there was a witness: the gamekeeper responsible for that land had seen what she was up to, and sent a man to retrieve the mutton. When the chunk was held against the roughly-butchered carcass later, it fit into place perfectly, and Sarah was arrested.

According to the *Lincolnshire Chronicle*, John Blades, the local policeman, had noticed distinctive footprints in the mud leading directly to a point just 300 yards away from the Carbys' dwelling and dug them up with a spade. When Samuel was arrested and his mother's house searched, his boots were found to match the marks in the mud and the paper gleefully reported that there was 'blood on his trouser's knee, also several spots on his slop frock and shirt wristband …a carving-knife was found at his house covered with blood and grease [and] his flannel jacket found on his bed was also very much greased'. Sarah was set free, on the condition that she bore witness against her fiancé. Carby later said that he had nothing to do with slaughtering the sheep, and had accepted the mutton as a gift before his wedding. In trying to dispose of the evidence, Sarah had only made things worse.

George and Samuel were both sentenced to ten years' transportation to Van Diemen's Land. They were held in Oakham Gaol, until they were shipped out from London on the *Gilmore* on 16 April 1843, arriving four months later in the middle of the Antipodean winter. According to the census, Sarah returned to her parents and they raised Robert as their own son. Sarah supported herself by making stays, and earned a reputation for respectability and good character. With Robert concealed as her sibling, she was a far more marriageable prospect, but she remained single until 1853, when Samuel returned home.

Samuel had worked hard and received a pardon six years into his sentence. Around this time the Gold Rush was beginning in neighbouring Australia, and eager for a new start, Samuel soon left for 'the diggings', the sites excavated for quartz and gold. The influx of rogues, thieves and miscreants, some of whom quickly reoffended, infuriated immigrants who had paid for their passage to the Gold Fields. They resented convicts travelling in search of a fortune courtesy of the tax-payers' purse, and this was one of the reasons for the gradual abandonment of the sentence of transportation to the Antipodes.

'Crime has been rewarded with golden chains. A glance at the system pursued will prove this fact. A highwayman or a burglar is sentenced to transportation for a term of years. After remaining for a limited period in a penitentiary or on board a hulk, he is transported to a penal settlement in Australia ... [t]he natural result of this system is that the convicts flock to the gold fields'. The *West Kent Guardian*, one of many newspapers calling for an end to transportation, remarked in 1853:

> [*Here*] *it is to be feared they will find a focus of attraction, and a centre of union which they never possessed before.... These are not idle fears when it is considered that four thousand criminals are yearly sentenced in England to transportation, and that no large military force exists in Australia.... We cannot afford to stimulate the commission of crime by raising its recompense above that of honest industry, or to peril the social well being of our relatives and friends in Australia by the unwelcome visitation of the refuse of our population, and the most hardened of our criminals.*

Luckily for Samuel, he reached the Gold Rush early and somehow struck it rich. On his return home to Stamford, Samuel settled the vast sum of £600 (equivalent to over £40,000 today) – on Sarah, before taking her to London to arrange his affairs with the Australian bank. They used more of Samuel's fortune to purchase boxes of boots and other items that were difficult to obtain in the diggings, married, and arranged their trip back to the Gold Fields. The reunited family had intended the freshly fitted-out *Tayleur* to transport them to a prosperous future. They had been lucky to survive the shipwreck, but all their goods and the 200 gold sovereigns Sarah had sewn into her corset were lost forever. As their scraps of clothing steamed in the warmth of the cottage, sweat mingling in the damp air with the sweet smell of smouldering peat, perhaps like many of the other survivors the Carbys were simply thankful to be alive.

Meanwhile those with cuts, scrapes and bruises were packing the straw onto the sodden grass in the hollow behind the cottages and securing a makeshift wall of luggage and spars against the gusts of wind still blustering across the island's exposed fields. The huts and cottages were small, cramped dwellings, not large enough to accommodate more than a few guests at a time, and the castle was only the size of a big house. The emigrants and sailors tried to sleep, shuddering in the extreme cold, and as passenger Edward Tew recalled, 'The night was dreadful; we were almost starving; many of us were nearly naked and wet through'.

Despite the rough weather, chief coastguard George Finlay couldn't rest until he had made an attempt to rescue the man abandoned in the rigging. Once the storm had died down a little and the tide had receded so it was no longer rushing into the cove, the coastguard approached the wreck of the *Tayleur* in a boat. At 2 am Thomas Willet helped retrieve the last man alive on the *Tayleur*, who by this time had spent 14 hours clinging to the rigging 'without food, and exposed to wind and weather'. Willet said later:

> *I saw him afterwards, and asked him if he did not suffer from the cold. He said he kept working his hands and feet to keep warmth in them; but that when night came on he occasionally fell asleep from fatigue and cold, and was awoke from time to time by the cold, when he renewed the motion and working of his limbs.*
>
> *At last, overcome, he fell fast asleep, and so was found by those who took him off, and who had to call loudly to him several times before they could awake him. He said that an hour or two after we left him alone, the scene became most horrible. The bodies rose again, and scores were visible in all directions, floating about on the surface of the still heaving sea, – husbands and wives, parents and children, clasped in each other's arms, and he saw several mothers, whose last convulsive clasp was still rigid around the lifeless limbs of their infants.*

The last survivor on the *Tayleur*, William Vivers of Dumfries, had made it through the ordeal by shrouding himself with the torn remnants of sails still above water. As the thick white canvas flapped in the wind, he climbed down the rigging with stiff fingers and sore limbs, then grabbed the line thrown across to him by the men in the boat. He was pulled through the water and over the side of the coastguard's vessel, soaked through once again, but safe at last. As Vivers later recalled, the coastguard's wife got out of bed to look after him when he finally entered her cottage. Although shipwrecks were then commonplace, and people living on the coast were well used to finding the beaches covered with detritus and dead bodies, the population of the island quadrupling overnight was still a shock. The grace under pressure shown by the inhabitants of Lambay was laudable.

A few hours later, before it was fully light, the sea was calm enough to allow first class passenger Thomas Kemp to hitch a ride with the coastguard as they crossed the few miles of sea to Rush to gather fuel, food and other supplies. He hired a car (a private horse and carriage) and travelled to Dublin to break the news of the tragedy to an insurance agent with Lloyd's, the *Tayleur*'s insurers, who immediately made preparations to send a steamer to collect the rest of the survivors.

Around that time, according to the *Bristol Mercury*, Edward Folwell, son of a hackney-cab proprietor, was also escaping the island, leaving his former servant the young widow Rebecca Chasey behind, having endured a difficult morning at the wreck site:

On going to the rocks on Sunday morning a sickening spectacle presented itself. I saw, of both sexes, full a hundred bodies in the clefts of the rocks. Many of them were naked, their apparel having been torn from them in the night, and some were so mutilated through having been beaten against the rocks that it would be difficult to recognise them. I assisted in raising some of them, which we did by lowering men on ropes, who attached lines to the corpses and thus enabled us to haul them up.

At about 11 o'clock on Sunday a fishing smack, which had been out four days beating under stress of weather, put in, and I and two others (first cousins, belonging to Meath, named John and William Porter) determined to avail ourselves of her, and after a short but rough voyage, we landed at Malahide. I had but 9s. in my pocket, but on my landing two kind gentlemen (whose names I am deeply anxious to learn) gave me [more] – one of them two sovereigns and the other 7s. With this we got on to Dublin, where we gave information of the wreck, and from that city Captain Burgess of the Rose *brought me to Bristol, kindly allowing me to travel best-cabin side for half-a-sovereign.*

While some, like Folwell, were eager to depart as soon as possible, other *Tayleur* survivors felt bound to stay and recover the bodies of their fellow passengers. Edward Tew, who had tried so hard to rescue a boy from the water, also helped to raise bodies from the shore. As he told the *Norfolk Chronicle*:

> *The next day was as bad as the day before. When we went to the wreck we found bodies piled over each other, all naked, and mangled in such a manner that no one could tell who they were. I helped some of the sailors down the rocks by a rope which was fastened round my waist. I then sat down and fixed my feet against a projecting piece of rock. In this way I could have supported a bullock, and of course the rope could not slip from my hold. I was obliged to remain in this way for an hour, every one declining to take my post; but one man was good enough to cover my feet with sods to keep the cold off. There was only one lady brought up the cliff, she was naked all but her stays, and had two diamond rings on her fingers. I was told about two hours after that some inhuman monster cut her finger off for the rings.*

The mutilated lady was 23-year-old Miss Catherine Webster, of Stamford, Lincolnshire. She had been travelling in a party of friends, a few of whom had survived. Among them were heroes. The *Stamford Mercury* celebrated their bravery:

> *The first to leave the vessel and gain the rocks were three foreign sailors; and the sixth was Mr Ashby, who descended by a rope, and helped to fasten it to admit of the escape of others. Ten men who followed him, however, were everyone lost, and the next who successfully descended was Mr Tebbutt, he having obeyed Mr Ashby's call to seize that opportunity of landing. Before Mr Ashby left the ship, Miss Webster begged him to save her, and he promised to do so, if possible, but immediately after she swooned, and was not again seen alive...*
>
> *When Mr Tebbutt reached the rock, he aided Mr Ashby in fastening the ropes to the rocks, and for nearly half an hour they were engaged in rescuing their fellow passengers, frequently at the imminent risk of their own safety, as the waves continually washed over them, and nearly carried them off*

their footing. While employed in their humane task, one of the ropes broke away the piece of rock to which it was fastened, in consequence of the weight upon it, there being at that time 60 or 70 endeavouring to escape by it, the whole of whom were cast into the foaming waters, and not one of them survived: they were dashed against the rocks and the ship's side, and there was no possible means of rescue for them.

Now Ashby, Tebbutt, Tew and many others began retrieving the remains of the people they had not been able to save. As the *Stamford Mercury* relayed to its readers:

The scene at the part of the coast where the accident occurred was a most horrible one to behold the next morning. No less than 47 corpses, all frightfully mutilated, were taken out of a creek: such had been the violence of the waves in dashing them against the rocks, that nearly all were in a state of nudity, their clothes being torn from their bodies; two or three were without heads; others had their limbs nearly severed; and some presented a still more shocking spectacle. We regret to add that, humane and intrepid as were some of the survivors, there were miscreants who plundered the corpses. Mr Ashby found the body of Miss Webster, and he buried it as well as he could, but one of her fingers which contained rings had been cut off. Altogether the catastrophe has been the most fearful one of the kind ever remembered, and it is easy to believe Mr Tebbutt when he states that it is impossible the awful scene can ever pass from his memory.

The two coastguard vessels each made three trips to the Irish mainland, returning with four sheep, several gallons of whiskey, and all the bread available in the area, courtesy of Sir Roger Palmer, a major landowner who lived nearby. Lord Talbot de Malahide, who owned the island of Lambay, sent further supplies with them, along with more men to offer assistance to the survivors. The *Stamford Mercury* reported that when Mr Howell, secretary to the City of Dublin Steam Packet Company, heard of the 'dreadful calamity' he ordered the *Prince*, the steamer captained by Thomas Dearl which had aided the *Scotland*, to retrieve the survivors, 'who were without food, and exposed to the danger of perishing from cold, hunger, and exhaustion'. Once the *Prince* had departed from the quay, it fell to those left behind in Dublin to sort food, clothing, lodgings and fresh straw for bedding for the passengers and crew of the *Tayleur*.

The crew of the *Prince* were absent, having left the docks to spend the Sabbath with their families, and the only other suitable ship was unable to make the journey until her boilers were refilled and her furnace supplied with fresh coal. An alternate crew joined Captain Dearl aboard the *Prince*, including the crewmen of the *Roscommon* steamer and a reporter from the *Freeman's Journal* who was desperate for a look at the wreck in spite of the dangerous white-capped waves churning the water between Dublin and Lambay. Dearl was on yet another rescue mission, having assisted those trapped on the wreck of the *Scotland* three days before. At 4 pm, with coffee heating in the galley and the boiler-man sweating over the coal, the *Prince* left her berth at the docks and made for the open sea.

The grey puffs of smoke from her chimney were soon lost in the clouds hanging heavy over the turbulent sea, as the *Prince* chugged towards the island. They intended to take the survivors on board and be back at the docks before midnight, but the raw weather further out to sea made this unlikely. She came into sight of Lambay at approximately 6 pm, to the delight of the survivors as they spied her safety lights glowing yellow in the dusk. However, first the *Prince* steamed closer to the wreck on the east coast of the island. Finding it to be just where the reports had stated and the weather still rough, Mr Kearns, the experienced branch pilot Dearl had brought with him, recommended returning in smaller vessels.

After stopping half-a-mile from the harbour, Captain Dearl decided to lower three boats and travel to the island, find out how many survivors there were, and take them on board the *Prince* before sailing to Dublin. The night was wild and threatening. As the *Freeman's Journal* went on to explain:

Mr Allen, Mr Brown, and the other gentlemen who went in the boats, accompanied by a portion of the crews, after landing and drawing their craft above high-water mark, proceeded across the island (about a mile and a half) to the creek where the wrecked vessel lay ... the waves breaking over her masts and rigging ... Immediately under the bows of the ship, in a narrow creek formed by the rocks at either side where the force of the tide converged, the strip of sand and shingle, where the shore is very steep, was found literally covered with dead bodies, both male and female, the remains of the unhappy creatures who had endeavoured to save their lives by letting themselves down by the bow ropes and bowsprit rigging, but who unfortunately were washed from their hold by the violence of the waves. Along the strand at either side of the creek the shore was literally strewn with dead bodies, and also with boxes, packages, and parcels, sea chests, &c. The remnant of the passengers and crew saved from the wreck were found encamped in the vicinity of the coastguard station. Several of the more respectable class of passengers had obtained shelter in the coastguard station house and in the few cottages adjoining. The great mass of the people rescued had bivouacked on a grassy hollow under the shelter of a hill, their encampment being fortified with boxes, chests, and parcels of bedding. All were found to be suffering many privations.

Passengers, such as William Jones from London, wondered why they were forced to remain on the tiny island, and begged to be taken to the mainland. They were desperate for relief from the wretched conditions there, and longing for hot food, dry clothes and a warm bed for the night, and also for a chance to let their loved ones know that they were alive. But Dearl had been talking to Noble, meeting him on board the *Prince* to discuss what had happened privately, over hot bread and coffee. The two captains agreed that the weather and the distressed state of the survivors made it preferable to wait for the morning before attempting to cross the dozen miles to Dublin.

The survivors spent another awful night either cramped in the island buildings or out in the open fields, as rain battered them where they lay uncovered on muddied straw. The whiskey from Sir Roger Palmer would have lulled some to sleep with a false warmth in their throats and bellies, and anaesthetised the wounded to a degree. Next morning the *Prince* steamed closer to the harbour through the dark. Her boats were let down into the water and moored in the harbour as the forlorn survivors massed on the quayside, preparing to travel by sea once again. According to the reporter from the *Freeman's Journal* still on the scene, they were 'speedily conveyed on board the steamer'. Despite the islanders' care:

The aspect of sufferers was deplorable in the extreme – all seemed [to be] suffering from cold, terror, and exhaustion, whilst many had their heads and limbs bound up, having received wounds, bruises, and injuries, more or less severe, by collision with the rocks, in escaping from the wreck. Too much praise cannot be given to Captain Dearl, of the Prince *steamer, for his prompt and effective measures in bringing off this multitude of sufferers from their forlorn and cheerless situation, and also for the care and kindness with which he caused their wants to be ministered to on board. On the arrival of each boat load the men, women, and children were divided into messes [it is more likely that the handful of women and children and their families were seated together] and were then accommodated comfortably in the after steerage, where abundance of hot strong coffee and good soup were distributed to all.*

Mr Walsh, an agent for Lloyd's, the *Tayleur*'s insurers in Dublin, assisted by Mr Allen of the Dublin Steam Company and other crewmen on the *Prince*, took down the names of the survivors and helped to make them comfortable. Once everyone who intended to travel that day was on board, Captain Dearl ordered the anchor raised, and the *Prince* proceeded at full speed to Dublin. Eventually the steamer arrived in her berth a little after 2 pm. The survivors crowded onto the quay and were shown to the Steampacket Company's office, where those whose name had been taken down on board the *Prince* were presented with a little money and a ticket for lodgings already arranged for them nearby.

The *London Standard* reported that:

An anxious crowd awaited her. The scene presented as she came alongside was most affecting. Almost every one inquired for was among the lost! Those landed looked wretchedly – many but half attired, having lost their hats and coats, and suffering from drenched clothing. Five poor fellows had to be sent to hospital. One fine specimen of a sailor, Patrick Bailey, had his arm broken in two places, trying to save a woman. Another, named Higgins, suffered a severe hurt in the leg while similarly employed ... The place where the Tayleur *struck is described as a little creek, with rocks jutting out at either side and in front. How so many managed to ascend the steep rocks*

that intervene between the water and the land can only be accounted for by
bearing in mind what a human being will attempt to preserve life.

Most of the passengers were now destitute, their goods and savings lost
on the rocks with the *Tayleur*, but a few had been lucky. Thomas Willet, a
passenger from Manchester, told the *Westmorland Gazette* 'there was one
singular exception. One young man was sitting with us, in one of the coastguard cottages, getting some thick porridge and butter-milk, when two girls
belonging to the cottage came in'. They had been out walking the coastline
and found a trunk washed up on the beach which they brought back to the
house. The young man immediately claimed it as his, though its time in the
water had stripped off the hair covering and therefore its identifying marks,
too. He took keys from his pocket and, stating it contained all his best clothes
and money, unlocked it, and 'raising a shirt or two, immediately drew forth a
sum of 501 [pounds]. from which he instantly gave the girls who had found
his trunk a sovereign each'.

Although most of the *Tayleur*'s child passengers had perished, one was
alive and well in the arms of an islander. The anonymous baby boy rescued
from the deck as the ship went down was as yet unclaimed, and his survival
was soon advertised in the press. The newspapers were eager to find the
child's relatives; his survival was seen as a miracle, and the public was keen for
the baby's story to have a happy ending. As the *Belfast News-Letter* reported,
'Probably the most singular circumstance which occurred throughout the
whole lamentable occurrence was the almost miraculous preservation of
an infant nine months old, whose parents had both perished in the sea'.
Captain Dearl refused to leave the baby on Lambay, assuring the islander he
would raise the child as a member of his own family, and 'the warm-hearted
woman displayed as much emotion on being separated from the infant as if
in reality it was her own offspring'. After two nights of nursing the baby, she
must have found it difficult to give him up. Captain Dearl had ten boys and
girls of his own, the youngest barely older than the anonymous infant, and
his household was ideal as a foster home. With the baby in his arms, Dearl
took to the sea, hundreds passing through the cabin for a look at what the
papers called 'The Ocean Child', as they travelled to Dublin.

Now only a few dozen of the most seriously injured survivors remained on Lambay, waiting for calmer seas before they were transferred to the *Prince*. With them were Captain Noble and some of his crew who were staying there to retrieve what they could of the goods the *Tayleur* had carried, and what was left of the bodies. A few personal possessions were labelled clearly enough to return to the survivors or the families of those lost, and some of the cargo might turn out to be salvageable and fit for resale. Thanks to their efforts, one of the passengers now on her way home was going to get a wonderful surprise.

Chapter Eleven

The difficulties of newspaper management require no aggravation; ... the eternal problem of pleasing all in a single sheet of paper, when half what you write offends your dearest friends, and the other half gives a handle to your worst enemy, and your temper is gird-ironed and your wit pumped dry, and your brains jellified in vain efforts to appease wrath, amuse levity, and convince stupidity...

A skinflint shipowner will withdraw every advertisement he can influence, and cut off your American news, if you presume to challenge the seaworthiness of the Tayleur; *what business is it of yours if two or three hundred emigrants go to the bottom? You are not one of them!*

(*Elgin Courier*, 28 April 1854)

Tuesday 24 January to Friday 7 April 1854, Dublin and Malahide

Had the tragedy occurred through sheer bad luck or through the negligence of the captain or owners, and if so was it indicative of a larger problem within the emigration trade? The newspapers, the public, and the authorities were all now clamouring to know the facts. The media, and by extension the public, might be satisfied with blame being attached to a few individuals or a single company, or perhaps new legislation would be required. However, it would be far cheaper and easier to find scapegoats unable to defend themselves.

When the investigator, Captain Walker, arrived in Dublin to examine the tragedy for the Government Board of Trade on 24 January, he went straight to the Jervis Street Hospital to interview John Nicholls, a *Tayleur* passenger and a professional seaman. Nicholls had suffered a severe dislocation of the foot while scrambling to safety on the rocks of Lambay and was recovering well. Captain Walker took down his statement under oath while the wind battered the windows of the hospital. Nicholls was no doubt glad to be safely inside while reliving his ordeal.

This was the start of the official Board of Trade inquiry into the sinking of the *Tayleur*, an investigation that was to merge somewhat with the coroner's inquest three days later. Four inquiries were arranged over the next few months, none fair or impartial by modern standards, though the press heralded the jurymen as intelligent and capable. But first, in a gesture the newspapers publicly interpreted as generous, the majority of the survivors were sent to Liverpool, with a handful remaining to give evidence.

While the weather prevented all but the most hardy souls from crossing to Lambay and viewing the dead, Captain Walker spoke to survivors still in hospital. He also awaited evidence from the *Tayleur*'s representatives, and spoke with the coroner, who was preparing for the inquest at Davis's Hotel in Malahide. Ideally, the inquest would have taken place on Lambay, allowing the coroner and jurors to view the site of the wreck, but the weather was too foul to risk boatloads of the local great and good foundering on the waves.

Despite the cold January air, the *Tayleur* dead were described by the *Hampshire Telegraph* as 'mouldering in heaps' in the island graveyard. In the end, it was agreed that three of the most easily recognisable and least mutilated corpses would be transported to the mainland, proceeding on two boats in case one of the vessels met with an accident in the rough seas. On 26 January, two sodden bodies were stacked in a hearse, which then delivered them to the hotel for official identification. Dr Cunningham's four-year-old son, last seen alive in his father's arms before the waves swept him away, was laid out alongside second mate Edward Kewley, who had met his end swimming for the rocks beside his captain.

The corpse of a boy with a wooden leg had also been brought to the mainland as back-up. Seven members of this child's family had died in the wreck, and his 17-year-old brother, William Jaffray of Dundee, had been the only one of the group of nine to make it to the clifftop alive. The boy wasn't immediately identified in the press, but there is mention of a child of about that age with an amputated leg belonging to this family, which narrows him down to either 12-year-old John or 10-year-old Graham Jaffray. It is unclear which one had the wooden leg. The boy had survived a major operation without effective anaesthetic, only to drown on the way to an adventure of a lifetime.

Captain Walker later reported to the Board of Trade that the coroner told him to ask any questions he pleased at the inquest, as there was 'no nautical person present to explain parts of the evidence'. Given that the inquest was taking place in a coastal town near the busy port of Dublin and was a high-profile inquiry into a shipwreck, the lack of jurors and board members familiar with sailing seems very odd. It was not the only suspicious absence at the inquest. Not one person attended on behalf of Charles Moore & Co., the ship's owners, nor from the Bank Quay Foundry, where the *Tayleur* was made. As for the underwriters of the ship, only a man called Jones attended from Liverpool, and he claimed he was there in no official capacity, purely 'out of curiosity'.

Even with the arrangements for the inquest widely advertised in the press, Captain Noble's solicitor and this mysterious Mr Jones attempted to delay matters by claiming there had been confusion over the location of the inquest. Noble's solicitor had apparently been waiting at Ringsend, where the third body was being held in reserve. Oldham, a solicitor acting on behalf of the merchant community whose goods had been transported on the *Tayleur*, pointed out that Captain Noble and the first mate had been at the hotel all morning. Jones claimed the men were never there, despite other witnesses describing Jones calling the crewmen away from their glasses of ale at the bar. When the head constable then stated that the captain, mate, and some of the crew had just left town in a horse-drawn taxi, Jones could no longer deny their earlier presence in the hotel. Nothing much was made of this, either in the formal reports or the newspapers, but it seems clear there was something strange afoot.

Eventually, after much persuasion, the coroner issued summonses for Captain Noble and his shipmates, and the business of the inquest finally began. Surviving passengers, including John Aislabie, whose wife and four-year-old daughter had been lost in the wreck, described an ill-disciplined mess of a ship, where the foreign crewmen could not understand their orders, and the deck was covered in coils of rope too new and thick to easily use. All this, they argued, had added to the chaos when the ship hit the rocks. Aislabie also told of Noble's apparent confusion when they reached the clifftop, remarking that he could only attribute the captain's request for dry matches to ignorance of the ship's location.

When the inquest resumed the next day, the captain and his crew were present. Mr Coffey, counsel for the merchant community, argued that if Noble was examined first, then all the other witnesses should be put out of court, as members of crew present might be unduly influenced and take the same line as Noble when questioned. The jury wanted to hear Noble's account last, but Coroner Davies said he considered the captain to be the most promising source of information and decided to examine him first. The coroner did, however, agree that the mates and crew were to be put out of the room while Noble spoke.

The young captain told of the increasing disparities between the compasses, his inability to take a reading using the sun or the stars due to the bad weather obscuring the horizon, and his complete satisfaction with the ship and his crew. Noble completely denied that there had been any issues with the crew, contradicting the evidence of the passengers, and would not hear a word spoken against his men. He spoke very carefully about the compass arrangements and his requests to the compass manufacturer to check and recheck them. He mentioned the possibility of a fault with the rudder and his opinion that the masts were not in the right places. Noble also said he thought the ship was very slow to handle.

Then the jury and Mr Coffey started to cross-examine Noble about his appointment on the *Tayleur*, and whether he had spoken with the charterers of the voyage. This prompted Mr Fitzgibbon QC to object, and choose this moment to announce that a subscription list to raise money for the survivors of the *Tayleur* had opened in Liverpool and already raised £2,500. In addition, the owners of the *Tayleur* would grant free passage to any passengers – but apparently not crew – who wanted to claim their money.

Noble faced possible prosecution for manslaughter and criminal negligence, as well as the destruction of his career. His new wife's father had cut her out of his will for marrying without his consent, and she was now wholly dependent upon her husband. His brother, Thomas, was also a ship's captain and any scandal associated with John was likely to have implications for him. John Noble was under tremendous pressure, but he was an honourable man. If he had wanted to avoid censure, he could easily have blamed the foreign crew, as the witnesses and press clearly desired him to. Yet, despite multiple witnesses claiming otherwise, he stuck with his story over the following days.

When it was Captain Walker's turn to be examined, he told the packed room of the scientific examination Noble had passed with flying colours before Walker's colleagues at the Board of Trade. He also explained the differences in legislation between naval vessels and privately-owned ones such as the *Tayleur*, pointing out that with non-naval ships there was no rule or custom for compasses to be adjusted (checked and re-magnetised) after taking on passengers and cargo, though he felt that the rules should be changed.

Then first mate Michael Murphy spoke, confirming that Captain Noble's rewritten copy of the lost logbook was accurate. The coroner was on the point of dismissing him when Charles Barry, acting as counsel for the Carmichael family of Glasgow, who had lost relatives in the wreck, interrupted, stating that he had some questions to put to Murphy first. Under examination, Murphy's evidence seemed to contradict the captain's account. However, the first mate had been out of the room while Noble discussed the crew and passengers and running of the ship, and was not to know that. Michael Reidy, the passenger who had told the previous day of his conversation with Noble about the crew, was now recalled for further examination. He stuck to his story, as did Holland, another passenger whose evidence was at odds with Noble's, despite the captain protesting "I deny every word of it, he must have mistaken me".

With the evidence reduced to the passengers' word against that of the captain and no progress to be made, Coffey moved on. He wanted to hear Nicholls' statement. This seemingly innocuous request prompted an odd exchange between the main parties posing questions at the inquest. Fitzgibbon, representing Captain Noble, was keen for the inquiry to close as soon as possible, urging that once the jury was satisfied with the explanation of how the accident happened and had decided whether any parties were criminally liable, that should be the end of it. Captain Walker was also loath to discuss Nicholls' evidence, and after further argument, one of the jurors stated that they were "perfectly satisfied of the compasses being wrong and as to how the vessel was lost".

Perhaps that should have brought the inquest to an end. But then Mr Coffey said that if they could not hear Nicholls' evidence at the inquest, then the jury should go to the hospital to hear it from Nicholls himself. The coroner could have called things to a halt, however he read out Nicholls' statement to the crowded room instead. Nicholls had been a cabin passenger on the *Tayleur*, and as a skilled seaman with experience on a variety of vessels, his testimony was expert and invaluable. Like the evidence of the other passengers and the chief mate, it also contradicted Captain Noble. Nicholls had noted his puzzlement that none of the experienced seamen travelling as passengers on the *Tayleur*, like himself, were engaged by Noble once aboard, as there were clearly problems with the crew and the ship. He commented that: 'there were many seafaring men aboard [as] passengers who would have willingly done duty, as well as many passengers who could have given much assistance; [and] is under the impression that another of the survivors, at present in Mercer's hospital, offered to engage with Captain Noble but was refused by him'.

Nicholls stated that he had gone on deck on the morning of the accident and found the captain standing 'evidently from his manner looking out for land'. He asked the man at the helm how long the *Tayleur* had been kept on the one tack, and was told the ship had been running in a straight line for the last 14 hours, which worried Nicholls, as by his calculations that meant they must be nearing Dublin. The water near Dublin was littered with wreckage from other vessels caught on the rocks and sandbanks not far from shore. This was where the *Scotland* had foundered just a few days before. Nicholls was sure they were in danger, and that the safest thing to do would be to turn the ship about and sail in the opposite direction, but he didn't feel he could approach the captain with his concerns. He 'was afraid of offending him, as his interference was contrary to the usual etiquette towards the person having control at sea'. After so many years spent on ships, this respect for the chain of command, and a healthy fear of mutiny, would have been ingrained. Nicholls went on to say that in his opinion, the ship's compasses were correct. He had compared them with two of his own, as did 'a French gentleman'. Fitzgibbon sneered at this last observation, stating that he did not think Nicholls' comparisons between compasses 'of the slightest interest'. The coroner offered to adjourn the inquest to allow the jury to examine Nicholls, but no one spoke up.

Then Coffey brought Mr Cutts, a passenger from Hull, whom he introduced as 'an important witness', to the stand. Cutts declared himself familiar with how sea vessels worked, before stating that in his opinion "the crew were inefficient; before the accident occurred at all the passengers were constantly talking about it". The coroner half-heartedly offered to adjourn the inquest, while also stating that he thought the jury had already made up their minds. Predictably, Fitzgibbon objected that he "did not see what good could arise from adjourning the inquest; for supposing every passenger on board the *Tayleur* were produced and gave similar evidence to that already given; it would not warrant the coroner in sending the captain or any of the officers to jail". A dramatic statement, especially since there had been no indication whatsoever from the coroner or the jury that criminal convictions might arise from the inquest.

Mr Coffey responded that it "most unquestionably" would not, but if the jury considered the crew had been insufficient or incompetent then they might conclude that there was "negligence on the part of the owners". There was further discussion among the counsels, and the jurors voiced their impatience at the delayed arrival of documents containing particulars of the crew. Finally one juror asked "Are we to wait here for another month then?" Fitzgibbon slyly commented that it didn't "appear that they would ever be forthcoming", which seemed to provoke the opposite reaction to the one he hoped for. The foreman of the jury declared them "unanimous in wishing to adjourn".

After the jury spent the Sabbath mulling over the evidence already laid before them, the room at Davis's Hotel filled once again for the third day of the inquest. The papers concerning the passengers and crew had arrived and were now pored over in detail, and George Finlay, the heroic commander of the coastguard, was also examined about the conditions at Lambay on the day of the wreck. He spoke of the poor visibility, heavy seas and gale blowing over the island, echoing Captain Noble's account of the weather.

Next to be questioned was Lieutenant Prior RN, first assistant emigration commissioner of Liverpool, who had first-hand knowledge of this stretch of the sea and over 40 years' experience in sailing. He had already given evidence to Captain Walker for the Board of Trade investigation into the tragedy, and would have been aware that his conduct was under as much scrutiny as that of Captain Noble. Prior stood by his actions, and those of the captain, stating for the record that he did not think a trial trip had been necessary, and that he went on board the day before she sailed. "It is my business to see that the crew were sufficient...I was perfectly satisfied with my examination of the ship...The only opportunity I had of knowing whether the crew could reef or steer was by their answering my questions". Lieutenant Prior claimed to be unaware "that any difference of opinion exists among nautical men" on the subject of how many crew should be allotted to a new ship under the regulations, which was extremely unlikely given his position in the thriving port of Liverpool and years of experience. He also appears to have chosen his words carefully when describing what he saw during his final inspection of the *Tayleur*, maintaining that he did not notice the brand new ropes. Given the passengers' descriptions of fresh ropes coiled on the deck, it would have been hard to miss them.

"In my opinion the vessel was in every way fitted to leave port, with crew, passengers and cargo. I never saw any ship better fitted. I consider that the crew were perfectly competent and sufficient to work the vessel", he concluded. Lieutenant Prior could hardly have claimed otherwise, as he had signed the certificates allowing the ship to leave on time. Considerable pressure would have been brought to bear on him if he had required the ship to delay its departure again. The passengers, crew and various officials in the port would have been unhappy, as would the ship's agents and owners to whom a delay would have been embarrassing and expensive. In addition, if Prior testified that the ship had been in any way deficient in terms of crew numbers or experience, he – and his employers – could be found liable for the loss of the *Tayleur*, as well as her owners and agents, so he spoke with caution.

Lieutenant Prior told the jurors that he saw nothing wrong in Noble having kept to one course for 14 hours, depending on which direction the ship was heading in. This should have settled any concerns the jury might have had about the ship's course after the evidence of John Nicholls. However, a juror then asked about the sounding of the lead (dropping a weighted line overboard and measuring how deep the water lay there). The

Tayleur had several depth charts for the area, allowing the captain and crew to plot courses avoiding known hazards, including sandbanks and treacherous currents, and work out their location according to their depth, should they be blown off course. Lieutenant Prior's evidence left no room for doubt that in not sounding the lead Captain Noble had made a grave and obvious error. It was standard practice to sound the lead especially if a vessel's location was in doubt or a ship was approaching land. He also stated that special compasses were available for iron ships, and that Mr Gray, who had provided the compasses for the *Tayleur* and adjusted them the day before the *Tayleur* left port, was "a first rate man in his business".

Captain Noble was questioned further, and answered every query about his position throughout the first part of the voyage clearly and confidently. He also told one juror, "I do not consider I stayed too long on one tack; with a fair wind that tack would have brought us almost to the equator". As the ship had apparently proved hard to handle, with stiff ropes too thick to move freely and a slow response to the wheel, this would have made sense if the compasses were working. Noble explained that he had not sounded the lead because he had thought he knew roughly where they were, and with the wind fresh in the sails and plenty of daylight, he had not deemed it necessary.

Significantly, Mr Coffey asked Noble how he had decided which crewmen were to be sent away from Lambay after the wreck and which were to stay with him to help salvage items and pull bodies up from the shore. Those who returned to the mainland were, unless badly injured and requiring treatment in hospital, free to return to Liverpool with the passengers, or sign up as crew on another ship. Noble denied that he had had any hand in choosing who stayed or went, but admitted that he thought there were "only six lost of the whole crew". The high survival rate of the crew compared to the passengers, especially the women and children, was barely touched on in the inquest or the newspapers at the time. Given that the inquest was held in part to satisfy the concerns of future customers of the shipping companies whose conduct and regulations were under scrutiny, this casual acceptance of the unusual fatality rates appears rather odd.

Noble also said he had not been aware of "any hole in her bottom; the water got in through her deck", another point never followed up. If his explanation was correct, then shutting the hatches and operating the pumps should have kept the *Tayleur* afloat. The fact that neither he nor the mates issued this order, nor shut the hatches themselves, could have arguably led to charges of inefficiency and negligence being laid against Noble. But no one commented. Once Noble had explained to the jury that he had managed to save "not a particle" of his own goods, and that the *Tayleur* was only partly insured, the board of 'learned men and highly intelligent gentlemen' turned their attention to Captain Robert Kerr RN, the government emigration agent based in Dublin.

Captain Kerr's evidence was damningly precise: "In Channel water it was Captain Noble's duty to take soundings repeatedly, and the oftener he does so the better he would secure the safety of the ship". He agreed with Captain Noble that he had been justified in sailing for 14 hours in one direction "because by his own account he thought he was going down the Channel". Nevertheless, he argued that if Noble had taken any soundings then he would have realised what his actual position was, and that there was something amiss. In that case, with a ship that would not obey her helm, Noble's duty would have been to return to Liverpool. But, as Dr Gibbon pointed out when summing up, if the compasses were wrong and the poor weather had prevented Noble from taking a reading using the sun and the horizon, how was the Captain meant to know what direction to take for home? Captain Kerr also thought the rudder must have been defective and argued that "an American ship would have carried fewer hands". As far as Captain Kerr was concerned, Noble had done "everything that prudence and good seamanship would dictate".

Then Coffey addressed the jury. According to the *Dublin Evening Mail*, he remarked "the circumstances under which this vessel was lost were very peculiar". He urged the jury to "express in strong terms" their disapproval of the ship-owners' mercenary arrangements that were "wholly directed" at having the *Tayleur* ready to sail on the appointed day, rather than taking measures to keep the large number of people on board the ship safe. They had "hurried out to sea a vessel so ill provided and ill prepared", he claimed. Coffey maintained that the *Tayleur* had been "manned by an inefficient crew" and accused the owners of "culpable negligence". He considered Captain Noble to have given his evidence "in a straightforward manner, and without any desire to conceal the truth or avoid the responsibility which he had unfortunately incurred" – a strange statement given that some of Noble's evidence had been at odds with that of passengers and crew. Yet, he argued, Noble still held "part of the responsibility of this terrible disaster" alongside the owners of the *Tayleur*, who had offered no evidence or assistance. He went on at some length about the evidence, before reminding the jury that their actions could "compel the adoption of future precautions for the preservation of life and property at sea".

Dr Gibbon spoke on behalf of Captain Noble, impressing upon the jurors that the purpose of the inquest was solely to determine whether any persons were criminally liable for the loss of life in the catastrophe. Dr Gibbon declared that the owners were in no way guilty of neglect, and reminded the jurors that the compasses had been examined shortly before the *Tayleur* left port and that she had been supplied with a full complement of crew, who were both competent and efficient.

The coroner told the jury that there could be no doubt as to the cause of death for the second mate and the doctor's son, and that there had been a great deal of evidence regarding the inefficiency of the crew. He noted that Captain Noble had testified under oath about the ship and her crew being in order, and had made no attempt to shield himself by diverting any blame on to the *Tayleur*'s owners or crew. Before the jury retired to consider their verdict, the coroner had one last statement to make – that as far as he was concerned, no criminal charges could be made against the captain. Captain Noble, his counsel and the relatives and friends of those whose bodies still floated in the sea a few miles away from the hotel prepared for an anxious wait.

After only a couple of hours, the jury delivered their verdict. They found that 'this deplorable accident' had happened due to the 'highly culpable neglect of the owners' in allowing the *Tayleur* to leave Liverpool 'without her compasses being properly adjusted' or undertaking trials at sea to learn 'whether she was under the control of her helm or not'. They also found fault with Noble, and stated that he 'did not take sufficient precautions to ensure the safety of the vessel by sounding after he found the compasses were in error'. The jury mitigated this by saying that the captain had 'acted with coolness and courage, and used every exertion in his power to save the lives of the passengers, not having left the ship until she was completely under water'. They also strongly recommended a change in regulations so that all emigrant ships, whether chartered by the government or not, would have the same number of men crewing them and the same precautions taken.

The media had followed the case closely, and the verdict was reported around the world. The *Freeman's Journal*, whose reporter had travelled to the scene of the wreck and witnessed the survivors' plight, criticized Captain Noble for his 'neglect in not sounding' after he had discovered the failure of the compasses. As they pointed out, if he was 'unable to make observations from the cloudy state of the weather, it was at least in his power to sound; and, with the land sighted in half or three-quarters of an hour before the vessel struck, he should have been more cautious'. The paper admitted, 'It is hard to speak harshly of a man who behaved with so much courage, and discharged his painful duty to his ship and freight with so generous a disregard of his own safety'. But they still remarked that if the *Tayleur* had been 'tried for one day in a brisk gale, the disorder in her compasses would have been discovered, and the other impediments to the working of the rigging corrected after detection'.

The paper's negative comment that the *Tayleur* had not been tried in rough weather was deeply unfair. Liverpool was a busy port with a lot of marine traffic, and with speed of the essence, it was impractical for new ships to wait for foul weather for a test run. This was not an isolated remark. Amongst the back and forth of questions, answers, inaccuracies and opinions, came a lot of unreasonable criticism. This included the fact that the ship was not trialled in the sea or the mouth of the Mersey, but there was no custom of doing this with emigrant ships at this time, and Noble had no reason to do so, since the *Tayleur* was a brand new and well-appointed vessel. Lieutenant Prior and Captain Noble had used the old regulations, not the current ones but this was not unusual either, especially in the port of Liverpool, and it was Prior who had had the final say on this, though Noble was pilloried for it in the press.

There were claims that the crewmen were insufficiently experienced, although a combination of seadogs and new recruits was common, as was a mixture of nationalities with varying comprehension of English. The *Tayleur*'s two or three Chinese crewmen still understood sign language well enough to get the job done, according to some of the survivors. Many people argued that when Noble had realised the compasses did not match he should have returned to port. However, visibility was too poor to allow him to work out where north was and take a reckoning, so there had been no safe way for him to steer for home. Captain Walker, having attended the inquest and gathered evidence through interviewing survivors and obtaining letters from the owners, stated in his report to the Privy Council for Trade that 'there must have been great blame or inefficiency somewhere'. He attributed the loss of the *Tayleur* to the faulty compasses, and Noble being unable to work out their location because of this. Walker also thought the wreck could have been prevented if Noble had sounded the lead, as protocol dictated when lost at sea with a cloudy sky, no landmarks visible, and an Admiralty chart to hand specifying the depths in the area. He commented that he found it 'extraordinary' that Captain Noble, who held a first class certificate and was 'recommended by the Liverpool examiners as an excellent officer' had left port in an iron ship without an azimuth compass on a voyage to the southern hemisphere, 'more specially when he admits in evidence that he had carte blanche from the owners to procure everything he wanted'.

Noble had made two grave errors in judgement, and despite his explanation of the weather being too rough for an accurate depth to be gauged and that there was no rule stating that he should have an azimuth compass on board, it seems to have puzzled Walker that such an accomplished seaman could make these mistakes. Captain Walker's report states his opinion that while the *Tayleur* had too few crew, no blame could be attached to them, nor to their language skills. He attributed 'great neglect and want of caution' to Captain Noble, though he also spoke highly of Noble's bravery and hard work: 'from the time the vessel left Liverpool until she struck upon Lambay, he appears to have been most active and energetic in his duties, seldom leaving the deck'. Walker acknowledged that after the wreck Noble did everything he could to help the passengers 'until the ship sunk under him and he had to swim to shore for self-preservation. Also during the inquiry he evinced the greatest desire to give every information required of him and gave his evidence in a straightforward manner, without a wish to disguise or conceal anything'.

Captain Noble's honesty was cited again and again in both the inquiries and the newspapers, but the evidence appears to contradict these assertions. Noble's integrity seems questionable, given the conflicting accounts at the inquests, but none of the other key figures appear blameless either. The report on the condition of the ship was written by John Grantham, surveyor of iron ships for the Admiralty. He and Charles Rennie, who had designed the *Tayleur*, examined the wreck with the help of divers on behalf of the underwriters. Grantham was also consultant engineer to the Bank Quay Foundry and he had helped supervise the building of the *Tayleur*, so it was hardly surprising when he reported that there was no possibility that design faults had contributed to the loss of the vessel.

The final inquiry regarding the *Tayleur* was held over a month later by the Liverpool Marine Board. A selection of magistrates and knowledgeable seamen gathered together to investigate whether Captain Noble deserved to have his master's certificate reissued. Noble had lost his copy in the wreck of the *Tayleur* and was therefore unemployable unless it was renewed. The panel consisted of men who had tested Noble for his original certificate and who were clearly on his side. Mr Townson, an Examiner in Navigation, remembered Noble well, 'I never examined anyone whose examination was more satisfactory'. He also described Noble's written account of handling a gale in his previous command as 'a masterpiece of skill', which Townson had later used as an example when delivering a lecture on sailing through rotatory gales. Captain McLeod, Examiner in Seamanship, spoke of his high regard for Noble from two previous examinations, and how he had recommended Noble for the command of the vessel he captained prior to the *Tayleur*.

After this complimentary build-up, Noble gave evidence to the board. He began by saying "I can only attribute the loss of the *Tayleur* to an error in the compasses", then recounted the efforts he had gone to in trying to make sure they were correct. He discussed the technicalities of the voyage at length, including his reasons for not sounding the lead. The chairman of the Marine Board Inquiry stated that the depth of the water by Lambay was near enough the same as the depth where the *Tayleur* was meant to be, so Noble would have been none the wiser anyway. Captain Noble admitted that all the hatches had been open as they approached the island, yet not one of the examiners questioned why the order was not given for them to be closed.

The third mate, carpenter and branch pilot who had towed the *Tayleur* out to sea were all examined, followed by John Gray, the compass manufacturer. Gray talked at length about magnetism, iron ships and his excellent reputation, before stating that 'an azimuth compass could be of no value in thick weather'. Noble had been castigated by Captain Walker for not taking one on the *Tayleur*, but Gray concurred that it was not usual for captains to have them.

Just nine days after this inquiry opened, Noble was found fit to captain a ship, and his certificate was renewed. While his name was technically cleared, the stain on Noble's reputation could hardly be forgotten, though he did have one newspaper on his side. His home-town paper, the *Kendal Mercury*, had spoken out on his behalf on 4 February 1854: 'Captain Noble gradually raised himself, by his activity and diligence and good conduct, to high repute as a sailor. He is well remembered in Penrith, and spoken of by all his acquaintances with the most pleasurable remembrances'. He was a local boy made good and the *Mercury* supported him, skimming over the more negative remarks about the validity of the inquiry in the national press, for example, that it appeared to have been 'little more than a hearing of that officer's account of the cause of the mistaken course of the ship, and his conduct', according to *The Examiner*, and reporting his exoneration joyously.

One thing was never raised throughout all four of the inquiries and thousands of newspaper articles on the wreck. It is something that would not have been considered at the time, but it could explain why an experienced and gifted captain at the pinnacle of his career might have misjudged simple things, including whether to engage the experienced sailors travelling as passengers. It may also account for Noble's unwise decision to approach the rocks broadside instead of head-on, and failure to give orders to close the hatches and evacuate below deck. If, as seems likely, Noble hit his head when he fell 25 feet onto the deck of the ship in Warrington, he probably suffered a traumatic brain injury (TBI). The effects of this would have been subtle and probably would have gone unnoticed until Noble was tired and experiencing stress, such as preparing for the highly-anticipated maiden voyage of the *Tayleur*, and going without sleep for over 48 hours.

Modern research finds that people with a history of TBI are 'susceptible to the effects of stress' (Hanna-Pladdy et al.). Symptoms can include processing information more slowly and struggling with memory and cognitively challenging tasks – all symptoms that Captain Noble arguably displayed leading up to and during the wrecking of the *Tayleur*. For example, Noble had previously demonstrated such able seamanship during a storm that his log was used as a teaching aid. He had battled storms and dealt with the typical crewing problems of the nineteenth century with aplomb, promoting his third mate on a previous voyage when the original second mate died at sea, and still achieving a record-breaking time for the trip. After the fall, he struggled with adequately manning the *Tayleur* despite the owners apparently giving him a free hand in hiring and experienced passengers offering him their services.

If Noble had thought more clearly, he could have ordered the hatches shut in the 20 to 30 minutes between sighting land and wrecking, or ordered those on deck to climb the rigging to save themselves once the ship had hit the rocks. He could have ordered the alarm raised amongst the hundreds of passengers below deck. But Noble did none of that, and it was left to Dr Cunningham and others in the crew, including Frazer the ship's carpenter, to organize those on deck and sort out escape routes for the passengers crowded there. Noble was unquestionably a brave and intelligent man, but he seems to have been in a state of confusion when he finally reached the clifftop, asking his companions for dry matches in the pouring rain.

Chapter Twelve

I made a visit last week to Lambay ... to identify, if possible, two persons from my own congregation of Alnwick, who were married only three weeks ago, and who I had every reason to believe had perished. ... On reaching this place, a truly melancholy spectacle presented itself – the naked and mutilated remains of seventy-six human beings, in almost every state of decomposition, lay before me ...

I visited this spot, if possible, to identify my friends, but I found it utterly impossible to do so. Had they been there, a brother could not have recognized a brother, nor a husband his own wife, the remains had been so much mutilated, many bodies without heads, and few being altogether perfect. Out of seventy-six bodies which were lying stretched out upon the grass, there were only six of those women. The bodies, when brought ashore were, with but a few exceptions, and these very trivial, quite naked. It was at first supposed that their bodies had been stripped by those persons living on the island, but this is not the case; there can be no doubt that the stripping was effected by the bodies being dashed against the sharp pointed rocks ...

I saw seven in a small creek, which were so jammed in the crevices of the rocks that all means to extricate them had failed. It is probable that many bodies, particularly those of women, are yet in the cabins of the ship, having been unable at the time of the wreck to leave their berths, owing to sickness or other causes.

(Letter from Mr Walker of Birkenhead, published in the
Liverpool Courier, 8 February 1854)

While the inquests continued, and news of fresh shipwrecks filled the front pages, the survivors of the *Tayleur* got on with their lives. Thirteen babies had died in the wreck, along with many of their families. But against all odds one baby dubbed the 'Ocean Child' and two other children from the 70 known to be on board survived. Soon after bringing the anonymous baby to the Irish mainland, Captain Dearl was due to return to sea. Instead of leaving the boy with his wife Harriet, he passed the baby to the Reverend John Hopkins Armstrong of Dublin.

Armstrong lived in a four-storey terraced house on Herbert Place, overlooking the canal with Isabella, his wife, and their five children. The eldest, Mary, was seven and the youngest, Jane, not quite a year old, and the Ocean Child was a welcome addition to the household. The Reverend was Chaplain of St Stephen's Church, a few hundred yards from his home. Born in Dublin in 1819, Armstrong's father had fought under the Duke of Wellington in the Peninsular War. He and his wife had both died young, leaving Armstrong an orphan, like the Ocean Child. Armstrong was raised by his uncle before attending the well-respected Trinity College, Dublin, and embarking on a tour of the Holy Land and some of the capital cities of Europe. An intelligent and educated man, he had no qualms about approaching the newspapers for help in tracing the Ocean Child's family.

Armstrong fielded queries from grieving relatives hoping their nephew or grandson had somehow survived, including the Thains of Elgin, Scotland, and the Moores of Broughshane, Ireland, and accepted donations to a fund set up to benefit the child. In a letter to the editor of the *Dublin Evening Mail*, the Reverend thanks a donor and mentions his visit to those still recovering from injuries received in the wreck. He also comments that at the time of the accident, 'the little fellow was evidently nursing, and has suffered from such an unprecedented manner of weaning. Dr Kennedy has kindly visited him, and thinks he will do well: he considers him to belong to the middle class. Perhaps some who read this would inquire for the foreigner with whom the child was first seen, and so help me in my endeavours to trace out its relatives'.

Armstrong placed advertisements in the local press, which were reprinted throughout the British Isles. The *Bath Chronicle and Weekly Gazette* printed the child's description on 2 February 1854: 'Boy, about twelve months old, unweaned, fine skin, blue eyes, dark eyelashes, light curly hair, square prominent forehead, two lower teeth, without any marks whatever on the body; of a lively affectionate disposition, and has apparently been much petted; supposed to belong to the middle classes'. Armstrong's efforts soon paid off. A surveyor called Mr Geraghty contacted him on behalf of the Ocean Child's grandmother – the baby now had a name, and a relative coming to take him home.

As the Reverend wrote to the editor of the *Dublin Evening Mail*:

> *It appears that he is Arthur Charles, son of Charles Griffiths, who had been formerly a servant in the neighbourhood of Hereford, and latterly kept a small shop. His maternal grandmother has come over to claim him ... she and all his relations are respectable people, of good character, members of the Established Church, and very poor. The old woman earns her livelihood by weeding in gardens and other similar work; consequently the subscription which I have raised will be most beneficial.*

Little Arthur arrived in Ross, Herefordshire, and was placed with a wet nurse. According to the *Hereford Times* he became 'an object of attraction to visitors'. The reporter noted, 'He is a lively and affectionate child, and from the way in which he clings to those who fondle him, it might be inferred that the horrors of the scene from which he was so providentially rescued, have left an impression upon his infantile senses'.

The kindly Reverend John Jebb, a Dubliner and friend of Reverend Armstrong living in Peterstow, near Ross, supported Arthur and his family, keeping an eye on the little boy and also maintaining correspondence with his former foster-father. Although Arthur's family were impoverished, the public subscriptions meant that he wanted for nothing and his family could afford to call a doctor when he became ill. Medical assistance was soon necessary, as Arthur was growing wan and listless at an age where most infants were learning to walk and talk. He had endured great trauma, travelling to Liverpool to board the *Tayleur*, being orphaned in the wrecking then passed from family to family, plus the long journey home to Ross, before he was even a year old.

However, it is hardly surprising that Arthur sickened. Dysentery, or the 'bloody flux' as it was often known, killed more young men than warfare at that time. In children it started with nausea, fever, abdominal cramps, vomiting and diarrhoea occurring sometimes hourly with blood, pus, and mucus expelled amongst the stinking mess of faeces. This, coupled with the vomiting, led to severe dehydration very quickly and often resulted in shock and death. Between doses of laudanum, the child might have been in agony but too dehydrated to cry. At the beginning of the disease little Arthur would have shivered and sweated, alternating between chills and fever, as his lips chapped and cracked and his eyes sank into his face.

Despite the money from well-wishers and the best efforts of a doctor, Arthur died a painful unpleasant death aged one year and five days, on 29 March 1854, just two months after his near-miraculous rescue from the cold Irish Sea. Reverend Jebb buried the tiny body in Peterstow graveyard on 1 April 1854; no stone marked the spot. His former foster-father broke the news to the interested public in a letter published in the *Hereford Journal* and various other papers:

It is with much sorrow that I have to announce to the many persons ...
who took a warm interest in the young infant saved from the wreck of the
Tayleur, *that the life then so wondrously preserved has just been closed ...*
Allow me just to state that sympathy for the ocean child was not confined to
the upper classes. While the wealthy and the titled contributed and offered to
adopt the child, the artisan, the mechanic, and the labourer ... sent me their
generous proposals, and, to their honour be it stated, offered to share with
him their hard-earned wages, and to rear him up as their own. He is now in
better hands, but may they receive their reward!

Public sympathy was also forthcoming for 28-year-old Rebecca Chasey, who had lost her husband and infant son in the wreck along with all their belongings. She initially returned to her family in Bristol. Rebecca's previous employer, Mrs Folwell, whose family ran a hackney cab company and whose son, Edward Folwell, also survived the tragedy, used her connections to raise funds for 'The Widow Chasey', as she referred to her in a message of gratitude to donors. They included all ranks of society, from Bristol's mayor to 'A little Girl', according to the *Bristol Mercury*.

Rebecca Chasey was one of the luckier survivors of the wreck. Not long after she landed in England she recovered most of her family's savings, which had washed up in a box containing her husband's Odd Fellows' ticket and £15 in gold. The Odd Fellows were a charitable group, a kind of trade union, savings club and health insurance scheme, in the days before free healthcare and sick pay. Fortunately, the person who had recovered the box was also a member of the society and was able to trace the ticket-holder back to the Bristol lodge.

Fourteen years later Rebecca married a widower, George Aldridge, and settled in Bedminster, Somerset. Ten years her senior, Aldridge had lost two children as well as his wife, but still had five daughters aged from 10 to 25. He earned his living as a boot-clicker, cutting leather with a noisy 'clicker' machine to make the uppers for shoes, while Rebecca became a chapel-keeper, a caretaker of the local church who secured and unfastened the church doors and readied the place for a service. She died aged 60 in 1885, her husband a few months later.

Ann Carty, one of the other two women to survive the shipwreck, vanishes from the records at this point. The only surviving female child, four-year-old Ellen Anne Rimes, who had been carried from the wreck in the arms of her father, Gabriel, was returned to her extended family in the hamlet of Marholm, Northamptonshire. She was raised by her mother's family on their farm, four miles from her old home, while her father returned to Liverpool and ultimately took the free replacement voyage provided to *Tayleur* survivors by the White Star Line, landing in Melbourne the following June. Ellen went to school then, according to the 1871 census, worked as a governess for the Bagshaw family in nearby Nassington. No more is known of her or her father.

The body of four-year-old Henry Thomson Hannay Cunningham was claimed by his uncle after the coroner's inquest and taken back to Scotland for burial. His mother, father and baby brother may have been buried anonymously in Ireland, or possibly their bodies were swept out to sea.

Edward Tew Junior, the banker's clerk from West Yorkshire, who tried so valiantly to save a child and helped retrieve bodies from the shore despite great physical discomfort, returned home after the wreck. According to the 1861 census, he married a Londoner, Anna Jelley, and moved to Alness, in the Ross and Cromarty area of Scotland. There he farmed 450 acres, and had seven children in quick succession. The 1871 census indicates that Tew's farm was a success, as by this time Edward cultivated 2,004 acres and employed 32 labourers, a farm manager and three boys. Ten years later, he was living as a gentleman in Dartmouth, in 'Gunfield', a grand old house by the sea and later followed in his banker father's footsteps by becoming a local magistrate. He died in 1899.

* * *

For a man named Thomas Considine, the wrecking of the *Tayleur* meant trouble with the law. According to an article in the *Morning Post*, a large sum of money belonging to the Provincial Bank in Ennis had been mislaid in December 1852 near Crusheen in County Clare. Considine belonged to a very poor family and had suddenly left town at this time, saying he was off to America, but instead 'took a passage' in the *Tayleur* for Melbourne. Then 'after arriving in Dublin he wrote home for some of the money'. Suspicions were aroused 'as it was well known that the family were distressed [impoverished]', and the authorities became involved. The unfortunate Considine was taken into custody in Dublin, and the trail in the archives ends there.

Thomas W. Lloyd, the man who sent a note home from the crowded deck of the *Tayleur*, did not make it off the ship alive. He was a retired fellmonger (dealer in hides and skins) from Evesham, travelling to Australia to see his son. His wife, to whom he wrote in such haste while leaning on the crown of his hat, received his letter after the *Tayleur* wrecked. She had not known he was on board that particular ship until it arrived.

Captain Noble, though a free man with his good name somewhat restored by the findings of the inquiries, would be deeply affected by the wreck. He had lost his clothing and possessions, but one of the coastguards found Noble's watch washed up on the shore and returned it. With his certificate now restored, Noble was given command of the *Earl of Sefton*, another new ship from the White Star Line owned by Pilkington and Wilson – just like the *Tayleur*. As an Australian paper, *The Argus*, reported in 1855, Noble subsequently had 'a most successful voyage' on the *Earl of Sefton*, gaining an enthusiastic testimonial from the passengers about his conduct on board and his sailing abilities.

Eleven months later, the *London Standard* stated on 21 December 1855: 'The Royal Mail ship *Earl of Sefton* ... will sail tomorrow forenoon for Melbourne, with the usual mails for the Australian colonies, about 180 passengers, and one of the most valuable cargoes which ever left the Mersey in one vessel on freight, being composed almost entirely of fine goods'. The trust demonstrated by his employers led Noble to be portrayed in the newspapers as a dependable captain. He repaid them by outdoing competitors' ships, according to an article in *The Empire*: 'The Royal Mail Ship *Earl of Sefton* ... has beaten every vessel which left for several weeks before her, including two noted London clippers ... both having sailed ten days before her, and the latter of which has not yet arrived. A very flattering address signed by all the passengers, accompanied by a very valuable telescope, was presented to Captain Noble on the arrival of the *Earl of Sefton* in the Mersey'.

Noble, still just 31 years old, was also gaining a reputation for kindness to passengers of every class. He took great care of all who travelled with him, in stark contrast to many less diligent captains of the time. *The Courier* reported in 1856: 'The passengers have enjoyed good health, and it is almost needless for us to state that Captain Noble has again won their esteem. Indeed, we have seldom visited a vessel where the commander and officers were spoken so highly of for their universal kindness, attention, and gentlemanly bearing towards their passengers'. As adverts for the *Earl of Sefton* in *The Sydney Morning Herald* boasted: 'Captain Noble's kindness and attention to his passengers are ... well known'. The *Tayleur* seemed all but forgotten, and any lingering health issues from Noble's fall in 1853 do not appear to have resurfaced. Noble's career was once again on the up, but the captain's luck ran out in 1859 when the *Earl of Sefton* was destroyed by fire at sea. Once again, his master's certificate was lost with the ship. There was however, only brief mention of this disaster in the newspapers at the time.

Noble's certificate was reissued on the sixth anniversary of the *Tayleur* tragedy, which is perhaps a coincidence, but at a stretch could be seen as a deliberate message from the authorities. He was then given command of the *Ocean Home*, following the same route from Liverpool to Australia and back. Another ship with the same name had sunk, losing nearly all aboard, after being run into accidentally by another vessel in 1857. The name did not bode well, but Noble captained the *Ocean Home* with his usual aplomb. He dealt swiftly with an outbreak of typhus among the passengers and crew, mooring at the Point Nepean quarantine station just off Port Phillip, Australia, in August 1860. Most of the passengers were released the same day following a medical inspection, while five were received into the hospital, with four confirmed sick with typhus. Spread by lice and fleas, typhus had reputedly killed up to 30 per cent of passengers on the so-called 'coffin ships' transporting poorer emigrants to America in the 1840s.

Noble managed the return trip back to England in October without further problems, and was preparing the ship for her next voyage when he became ill and was diagnosed with liver disease. He had apparently taken to drink some time after the *Tayleur* tragedy and this eventually made him sick enough to seek medical advice. His skin would have grown jaundiced from the liver disease, a constant source of irritation, and his skin and the whites of his eyes discoloured and unpleasant looking. He suffered through the winter, then developed dropsy in May 1861. Dropsy, now known as oedema, is a painful gathering of fluid in the soft tissues or cavities of the body, often evident as swelling in the limbs or abdomen or as breathing difficulties due to fluid accumulated around the lungs. It is usually a symptom of heart, kidney or liver disease. In Noble's case, it seems likely that his damaged liver was the cause of his distress.

Noble soldiered on, aware that the *Ocean Home* was scheduled to leave for Australia on 15 August, and keen to have the ship ready well in advance. But, as the fluid flooded his limbs and abdomen, he would have found moving problematic. His stomach may have grown painfully distended, the fluid within rippling in a wave if he changed position too suddenly. Breathing would have been laboured, resulting in his lips, tongue and eyelids turning blue. He would have struggled to leave the house as his organs ceased to function. Noble was trapped, seriously ill within shabby rented rooms in one of the less prosperous streets of Liverpool, four miles from the dock where the *Ocean Home* awaited his return. He died on 24 July 1861, with just a friend in attendance. He was 35. His body lies under a tree by a busy road in Toxteth Park Cemetery in Liverpool, memorialised by an enormous gravestone meant for a whole family, but with just his details summarised in a couple of lines inscribed below sculpted roses at the top.

Noble's cousin, Henry Bloom Noble, survived him, leaving a fortune to the Isle of Man, while Tom, John Noble's brother and fellow captain, died around the same time. John's wife, Anne Ray Noble, perhaps struggling with her husband's fall from grace and his drinking, had returned to her parents' home in Branthwaite, Cumberland, before his death. In 1868 Anne married John Hoppe, a travelling leather salesman. They had a son, John Ray Hoppe, two years later. Anne lived with her son, her husband and his father in Islington for a few years, before she was widowed in 1872. Anne married a third time on Valentine's Day 1874, to a soldier called William Fleming Cullen. He died in India three years later, leaving Anne a widow three times over. She died in the winter of 1899.

* * *

Former convict Samuel Carby and his wife Sarah Ann escaped the wreck with their son, 13-year-old Robert Bunning, and nothing but the clothes they had scrambled to the rocks in, their fortune of gold and goods still trapped in the wreck of the *Tayleur*. The Carbys returned to Stamford, Lincolnshire, in a small party of would-be emigrants, which included little Ellen Rimes and her newly-widowed father, Gabriel; Thomas Kemp, who raised the alarm with the agent in Dublin; and friends of the unfortunate Miss Catherine Webster, who drowned after she fainted on deck.

According to the *Stamford Mercury*, the Carby family were still keen to head back out to Australia and join the Gold Rush. But having lost the 200 gold sovereigns sewn into Sarah's underwear, along with the boxes of boots and other goods intended for sale at the diggings, they were unable to do so 'for want of funds'. Sarah's minister, the Reverend Joseph Place of St Martin's Church in Stamford, did his best to help them. He was 'aware of her exemplary character' and 'promoted a fund for their benefit'. Sarah also visited the local aristocrats at nearby Burghley House and was given money by Lord and Lady Exeter and their friends, once she had told them all about her terrible experience.

A month later, on 10 March 1854 according to the *Stamford Mercury*, Samuel and Sarah left Stamford for Liverpool and their replacement berths to Australia. They gave thanks through the paper to all those who had helped them to raise the money. The train fare to Liverpool and lodgings there, plus the clothing, bedding, eating utensils, luggage, shoes and so on cost a good deal. Even though their tickets were provided free of charge by the White

Star Line, it was still an expensive affair, the cost only reduced by the fact that Robert, who had just turned 14, was staying behind.

As the *Stamford Mercury* reported:

Another painful scene was witnessed at the railway station at Stamford on Friday last, on the departure of emigrants for Australia. Among the passengers were Carby and his wife, who with their son were saved from the wreck of the Tayleur. *It appears that the youth, since his escape from the wreck, has had an aversion to try[ing] another voyage, and could not be induced to accompany his parents. He went with them to the station, and there his mother renewed her persuasions that he should go with them: the lad, however, though much affected at the separation, resolutely refused, and when the time arrived for the train to start, Carby and his wife got into one of the carriages: the latter [Sarah] shortly after fainted, and in that condition was whirled off from her son and other friends who had assembled to wish the emigrants a more fortunate termination to their voyage than that in which they lost the whole of their property.*

The Carbys did not know it, but they and the rest of the *Tayleur* survivors on board the new emigrant ship the *Golden Era* had yet another narrow escape when they sailed in the spring of 1854. Twenty-eight-year-old James Tullis Peat was a well-regarded captain, the *Golden Era* another brand new ship heralded as clean and modern and this voyage to Australia was as pleasant as a long sea journey could be. However, the next journey from Liverpool made by Captain Peat and the *Golden Era* would end with a passenger in charge of the ship, Peat in custody, and the passengers and crew terrified and in need of a good meal. Apparently Peat had been drinking and abandoned his duties while the ship drifted through the ice-fields of the Antarctic and the provisions ran out. He refused to leave his cabin, even when the ship was in danger of becoming lost amongst towering icebergs and shifting channels, where routes could rapidly freeze up or become blocked off. His first mate was no better.

Eventually two passengers risked charges of mutiny and took over the vessel. Both were naval captains, and one of them, Captain White, ended up being appointed captain of the ship when they put in to a port in Pernambuco,

Brazil, for supplies. At this point, Peat tried to slip the cables and escape in the *Golden Era*. When this proved impossible, he ran the ship aground, gathered up the gold on board, and walked off with it, before being arrested and transported back to Liverpool to face a jail sentence of eight months and public disgrace.

Robert Bunning stayed in Stamford with his grandparents, Joseph and Mary Bunning, and trained to be a carpenter. He would have seen further newspaper articles relating to the *Tayleur* as he matured, including reports of decaying bodies from the wreck being washed up by the tide over a year later. There was little left to identify them, except in one case papers naming the *Tayleur* tucked into the remains of a waistband. Whenever they were found, the corpses were immediately given a respectable burial in the nearest graveyard.

Goods salvaged from the wreck that could not be returned to their owners were sold at auction in June 1854, including bales of clothes, carpets and blankets, 16 cases of window glass, lengths of wood and boxes of crockery. The wreck itself was also sold off, and no mention was made of the Carbys' fortune in sovereigns and boxes of shoes being recovered in the years after this.

Robert's parents returned to Lincolnshire some time before 1861, where they appear in the census of that year, Samuel recorded as a 'retired grocer' and Sarah as a 'stay maker', living in adjoining rooms to their son and his grandmother. Samuel and Sarah also ran a pub called the Leopard in Birmingham for a while. Yet, nothing about their lives suggests that the Carbys came close to repeating Samuel's earlier success in the Gold Rush. Robert married a woman from Birmingham, Elizabeth Smith, in Manchester in 1875, before settling in Rusholme. His descendants believe that he worked on the interior woodwork of the new Town Hall. Elizabeth bore a child a year before she died of meningitis in 1885, and Robert suffered another loss when his mother, Sarah, died aged 71 two years later. Samuel died near Eccles in the same place as his beloved Sarah in 1897 at the age of 79.

Robert raised his five small children with the help of his family and a housekeeper, before settling down with a woman called Sarah Ann Williams, who was 20 years his junior. They appear to have co-habited without ever marrying, and Robert had a further seven children with Sarah Ann between

1889 and 1898. Robert was bereaved once again when Sarah Ann died of a cerebral haemorrhage in 1900, at just 39.

Twelve years later the *Titanic* sank. The similarities between the *Tayleur* and the *Titanic* might have brought back painful memories of his escape onto the rocks, but he appears not to have shared them with his family. Robert's granddaughter was unaware of his childhood trauma on the *Tayleur* and the heroism and romance of Samuel and Sarah's story, so perhaps this was something he chose not to talk about. He survived the First World War before dying of bronchitis and heart failure in June 1919.

As one of the three youngest survivors, and with his mother among the three women to make it safely up Lambay's cliffs, Robert was lucky almost beyond belief. As Robert's great-granddaughter by marriage commented in 2013: 'It's sobering to think that none of them (Robert's dozens of descendants) would be here at all if Robert hadn't survived the wreck. He had 12 children and all their various offspring would also be non-existent. Life determined by a twist of fate…'

Afterword

This book made me cry. I had hoped that the process of writing it would allow me to lay the story of the *Tayleur* to rest, to answer questions through research, and make contact with descendants in order to establish a flesh-and-blood link with the events of that stormy January day. But, as is often the case when delving into the past, some questions remain unanswered. Here are a few of the issues that still niggle:

- **Samuel Carby** may have travelled to America and attempted to find a fortune to replace the one he had lost on the *Tayleur*. There are letters from a Samuel Carby in the Stamford newspapers which discuss emigrating for work and contacting a brother while out there, but no mention of a wife or child. This man could well be the Samuel Carby who survived the *Tayleur*, but there is not enough evidence either way as yet.

- **Captain Noble**'s headstone is a statement in itself. Huge and expensive, but mainly blank, I would love to know who paid for it and why. It has sufficient space for the details of several generations to be engraved below, or perhaps some kind of testimony to the high esteem Noble was held in, or the love felt for him by those he left behind. Instead, his name and occupation are carved along with his date of death, and the rest of the stone is bare.

Maybe his fellow captains or employers paid for it, or perhaps it was Noble's rich cousin, the ruthless businessman on the Isle of Man, who organised John Noble's funeral. I think it most likely that his father-in-law – who was, after all, a stonemason – was responsible, and used the gravestone to officially erase Noble's relationship with Anne Ray. I would be interested to know if the seven roses carved on the shoulders of this imposing memorial had any kind of meaning at the time, too. Roses generally indicated hope and love, and when in full bloom indicated the deceased had been in the prime of life.

- The mysterious '**Mr Jones**', who caused such disruption to the inquest before vanishing back into the ether, proved impossible to trace. It can be inferred that he was a white British man from the lack of comment on his race and accent in the reports of the time. Beyond that, he appears to have been connected with the shipping companies in some way. It is highly doubtful that he was a mere underwriter from Liverpool attending out of curiosity, having paid to travel in bad weather from England to Ireland just to see what was going on. The fact that he called the captain and crew away from their drinks at the bar as they waited for the inquest to begin next door, and sent them away in a hurry, perhaps to meet with someone to discuss what was to be said, is very odd.

- Eoghan Kieran, MSc, researched the '**patent rudder**' referred to by Noble and found no relevant patents lodged for rudders in the two years before and after the ship was built. Perhaps the patent was lodged before this, or maybe (given the unusual nature of the inquiries and the power of the parties involved) the paperwork was deliberately misplaced, leaving the ship owners free to deny responsibility in this matter.

- According to E.J. Bourke's research in *Bound For Australia*, **the Dockrell family** on Lambay were interrupted as they ate a meal by a man speaking a foreign language, who alerted them to the plight of those sailing on the *Tayleur*. One of the myths that grew up around the unfortunate events of the wreck is that the islanders initially approached by a survivor thought he was a 'devil' and refused to help – Bourke has disproved this and other myths in his book.

- **Thomas Considine**, the Irishman who found a bank's mislaid money and attempted to flee the country with it and start a new life, makes a brief appearance in the newspapers then fades back into obscurity. I wonder if he ever made it to America or Australia, and if he received a prison sentence or was transported to Australia so that he eventually made it to his chosen destination, albeit poorer than he had hoped.

- Despite my efforts, I could find no details of **Henry Thomson Hannay Cunningham**'s final resting place, which is probably somewhere near Crail, Fife. At some point I would dearly love to pay my respects at the graves and memorials of all the people involved in the wreck.

- It would have been satisfying to trace the descendants of the **heroic emigrant** who carried the Ocean Child to safety from the deck, or to at least identify him. Some accounts describe the baby's saviour as French, others German, but there are no names given in the newspapers available.

- Bourke's book contains an account, handed down through several generations, of **a child cared for by the Dockrell family** on Lambay for several years after the wreck. This cannot be the Ocean Child or Ellen Rimes, and since the majority of contemporary newspaper articles on the subject and inquest accounts detail three children rescued from the wreck, it's difficult to know what to make of this. Some of the survivors' accounts mention **another child** being brought ashore in circumstances similar to the Ocean Child.

There is every possibility that two babies were orphaned and only one retrieved from the cottages on Lambay as it was a period of great confusion and shock. But given how protective Captain Dearl was towards the Ocean Child, and how insistent he was that the child should be reunited with relatives, it can be assumed that if he had known of the child Dearl would have taken it to the mainland. Details in Bourke's book suggest another orphan child was raised there until it was about seven years old, when the family found out from a priest in Rush that the child had grandparents in Liverpool. However, this is difficult to verify and so I chose not to include it in the main body of this book.

I was struck by many personal resonances while I worked on this book. One of the crewmen has the same name as my father-in-law. Some of the birthdays echo those in my family. The description of the Ocean Child in the newspaper advert could have been that of my own cherubic little boy. The Carbys lived out their last days about an hour's drive away from my house, and Captain Noble is buried just a short train ride away. My family and I have visited his grave. Someday, on a calm summer sea, I plan to visit Lambay too, but when I do, I'll be wearing a life-jacket.

No matter how clear the sky or how blue the water, you can never be too careful at sea. When the *Tayleur* set out, 'the ship was good, the crew better, the captain best of all', according to *The Times*. 'The compasses were of the kind and quality supplied to the Queen's yacht – still, scarce had the *Tayleur* left port when she blundered upon an island on one side of a wide channel'. This book bears witness to the hundreds of hopeful people who lost everything when bad luck and biology combined with atrocious weather. When I visit the relics in their well-lit case at Warrington Museum, I'm glad I know more of the true story of the *Tayleur*. I'm also thankful to be on dry land.

Gill Hoffs,
Warrington, 2 June 2013

Acknowledgements

Support, tea, and cakes: Mike and Angus Hoffs (the former for his unfailing support, feedback, and cups of Guthrie tea; the latter for drawing bums on my notes and colouring them in with purple felt tips); Gloria MacLean (for traipsing round a wet Liverpool graveyard with her friends, macaroni cheese, and enthusiastic support); Lynne Otterson (for egging me on since I was little to write for a living – thanks mum!); Jim and Jean McGinn (for endless French toast, ketchup, and guidance as I grew up); Mia Avramut; Nick Dimmock; Laura Bogart; Jeremy Scott; Curtis Jobling; S.B. Phoenix; Dr Ronnie Scott; Adrian Lea (funeral advice); Michael J. Malone; Carolyn Roy-Bornstein MD (medical advice); Professor Diane Watt; Dr Heike Bauer; Pat Watt (cheerleading and chocolate); Ivan Walton; Dr Lynne McKerr; Brian Stone; Steve Weinman and *Diver Magazine*; Amy Gregor at brightsolid online publishing; Matt Potter of Pure Slush; Alex Cox; Dr Emma Briant; Jennifer Garside of Wyte Phantom Corsetry and Clothing; Eoghan Kieran MSc (for generously sharing his research, and expert knowledge of the wreck); Lynn Beighley; Mignon Ariel King; Jane Hammons; Andrea Mullaney (for suggesting I submit a proposal to Pen & Sword in the first place); Chloe Okholi; Colin Morgan (for discussing open hatches and accident investigation); Frank J. Fallon (for his wonderful cover art); Cheshire Cakes; Village Café; Daisy Cupcake Café; Nutella; Coraline Cat (for keeping my wrists and lap warm, and testing the limits of my laptop); Jen Newby (for being a supportive and kindly editor); Dr Amy Burns (who gave me my first big break and is a boon to writers across the world); Michelle Elvy; Iain Paton; and all the people I contacted who responded with such enthusiasm, support, and kindness to my often odd requests – including the records lady who didn't mind that I thought if you bought a birth and a death record for someone it would be cheaper, like a supermarket special offer.

More detailed thank-yous
Jennifer Garside of Wyte Phantom Corsetry and Clothing answered all my questions about clothing in the mid-Victorian era, and sent me copious notes, links and contemporary adverts and drawings on the subject. This was of enormous help to me when visualising the outfits worn by the women on board the ship, and exploring why so many may have died.

Craig Sherwood and his colleagues at Warrington Museum gave me a lot of information and also the opportunity to closely examine the *Tayleur*'s porthole, crockery from the wreck, and (most excitingly for me) the actual ribbon from the bottle of wine that christened the ship as she launched in Warrington. **David Moulding** deserves special thanks for telling me about the *Tayleur* in the first place and sparking the idea for this book.

Eoghan Kieran, the Director of Geo-Mara, kindly sent me his thesis and research material when I was in the final stages of editing this book, and proved an excellent source of additional detail and verification.

Michael Robbins at Harvard sent me information on the Hanna-Pladdy paper ('Stress as a diagnostic challenge for postconcussive symptoms', 2001) and was very helpful.

Nick McParlin, was of great assistance to me when I needed research and layman translations for the names of diseases in the nineteenth century, and read over my medical sections with a sharp eye and the online version of a red pen.

Descendants
Every relative I managed to trace and contact: Candy, Paul and Audrey Smith (relatives of Samuel and Sarah Carby, Robert Carby/Bunning); Jane Armstrong (Reverend Armstrong); Linda Lane (Reverend Armstrong); Lawrence Clarke (Captain Dearl); Kathy Fenwick (Anne Ray); Cynthia Mather (Captain Noble); Glenys Bell (George Bell, Samuel Carby's fellow transportee) – has been supportive of this book, and most were unaware of their ancestor's connection to the *Tayleur*. Candy Smith, the great-

granddaughter-in-law of Robert Carby/Bunning, has been particularly helpful and took the time to look up local records in Lincolnshire, proving an invaluable contact and one to whom I am forever grateful.

Museums/archives/historians/record offices
Craig Sherwood, Michael Roberts and Warrington Museum; Warrington Archives; Lorna Standen, Win Robinson and Herefordshire Archive Service; Wendy Thirkettle and the Manx Museum; Cynthia Dickinson of the Crofton History Group; Simeon Barlow and National Archives of Australia; Lorna Hyland and National Museums Liverpool; Andrew Campbell and Fife Family History Society; Dr Maire Kennedy and Dublin City Public Libraries; John Sharpe; Whitehaven Archive Centre and Local Studies Library.

Any mistakes or omissions are wholly my own. This book has only been made possible through the help and support of families, individuals, and institutions across the globe. Special thanks to Ancestry.co.uk and to the BritishNewspaperArchive.co.uk in particular, and the staff of Warrington Museum and Archives, who were unfailingly helpful, and whose display of *Tayleur* relics sparked my passion for the subject in the first place.

Bibliography

Bourke, E.J., *Bound for Australia: The loss of the emigrant ship* Tayleur *at Lambay on the coast of Ireland*, (Self-published, 2003).

Capper, J., *The Immigrant's Guide to Australia*, (George Phillip & Son, 1853).

Cawthorne, N., *The Sex Secrets of Old England*, (Piatkus, 2006).

Conolly, M.F., *Biographical Dictionary of eminent men of Fife of past and present times, natives of the county, or connected with it by property, residence, office, marriage, or otherwise*, (John C. Orr, 1866).

Corbett, J., *The River Irwell*, (Abel Heywood and Son, 1906).

Flannery, T., *The Life and Adventures of John Nicol, Mariner*, (Canongate, 1997).

Harvie, D.I., *Limeys: The Conquest of Scurvy*, (Sutton Publishing Limited, 2002).

Hayes, J.; Crosby, A., *Warrington At Work*, (Breedon Books, 2003).

Howlitt, W., *Land, Labour, and Gold*, (Longman, 1855).

Kieran, E., *The wreck of the iron clipper* Tayleur, (Archaeology Ireland, 2005).

Kieran, E., Tayleur, *A victim of technological innovation*, (Bulletin of the Australian Institute of Maritime Archaeology, 2004).

Larn, R., *Shipwrecks of Great Britain & Ireland* (David & Charles, 1981).

Mays, T., *The Victorian Undertaker*, (Shire Publications, 1996).

Rattle, A. and Vale, A., *Hell House & other true hauntings from around the world*, (Sterling Publishing Co., 2008).

Robinson, J., *Parrot pie for breakfast: an anthology of women pioneers*, (Oxford University Press, 1999).

Smout, T.C., *A Century of the Scottish People 1830-1950*, (Fontana Press, 1987).

Starkey, H.F., *Iron Clipper:* 'Tayleur' – *the White Star Line's 'First* Titanic', (Avid Publications, 1999).

National Newspapers and Periodicals

The Argus: 22 Oct 1852; 9 Sep 1853; 24 Sep 1853; 16 Jan 1855; 23 Aug 1860; 24 Aug 1860; 6 Sep 1861; 14 Mar 1936

Colonial Times: 3 May 1854; 27 Feb 1855

The Courier: 3 May 1854; 28 Jan 1856; 2 Apr 1856; 9 Apr 1856

The Empire: 22 Jan 1855; 22 Oct 1856

The Era: 12 Feb 1854

The Examiner: 4 Feb 1854; 6 May 1854

Freeman's Journal: 19 Dec 1850; 25 Jan 1853; 9 Nov 1853; 24 Jan 1854; 25 Jan 1854; 27 Jan 1854; 28 Jan 1854; 31 Jan 1854; 4 Feb 1854; 23 Feb 1854; 20 May 1854; 23 May 1854; 17 Jun 1854; 22 Jun 1854

The Lancet: Volume One, 26 Jan 1854

Life-boat: Volume 2, Issue 1, 1857

Morning Post: 14 Jul 1852; 6 Sep 1853; 24 Jan 1854; 31 Jan 1854; 7 Feb 1854; 14 Feb 1854

Reynolds's Newspaper: 4 Dec 1853

The Times: 3 Mar 1854

Local Newspapers

Bath Chronicle and Weekly Gazette: 11 Mar 1847; 2 Feb 1854; 13 Apr 1854

Belfast News-Letter: 13 Aug 1851; 25 Jan 1854; 27 Jan 1854

Birmingham Gazette: 30 Jan 1854

Blackburn Standard: 25 Jan 1854

Bradford Observer: 5 Jan 1854

Bristol Mercury: 28 Jan 1854; 1 Apr 1854

Burnley Advertiser: 10 Aug 1861

Bury and Norwich Post: 1 Feb 1854

Caledonian Mercury: 9 Oct 1848; 1 Jan 1857

Cambridge Independent Press: 4 Feb 1854

Carlisle Journal: 10 Feb 1854; 24 Apr 1860

Chester Chronicle: 1 Sep 1848

Cork Examiner: 16 Jun 1852; 22 Jun 1853

The Cornwall Chronicle: 27 Sep 1848; 25 Aug 1849

Cumberland and Westmorland Herald: 26 Dec 1998

Derby Mercury: 1 Feb 1854

Devizes and Wiltshire Gazette: 21 Jan 1847; 12 Jul 1849; 26 Jan 1854; 2 Feb 1854; 9 Feb 1854; 2 Mar 1854

Dublin Evening Mail: 27 Jan 1854; 1 Feb 1854; 22 Feb 1854; 14 Aug 1854

Dumfries and Galloway Standard: 13 Apr 1853; 26 Apr 1854

Dundee Courier: 14 Apr 1852; 20 Apr 1853

Dundee, Perth, and Cupar Advertiser: 2 Dec 1853; 24 Jan 1854; 27 Jan 1854; 31 Jan 1854; 10 Feb 1854; 17 Mar 1854; 28 Mar 1854; 26 Jul 1861

Elgin Courier: 29 Jul 1853; [G.S. in the *Liverpool Mail*] 28 Apr 1854;

Exeter Flying Post: 26 Jan 1854

Fife Herald: 2 Feb 1854

Fingal Independent: 30 Jan 2004

Glasgow Herald: 27 Jan 1854; 30 Jan 1854; 17 Mar 1854; 20 Mar 1854

Hampshire Telegraph: 28 Jan 1854

Hereford Journal: 9 Jan 1850; 1 Mar 1854; 5 Apr 1854; 10 Sep 1856

Hereford Times: 16 Apr 1853; 12 Nov 1853; 28 Jan 1854; 4 Mar 1854

Herts Guardian, Agricultural Journal, and General Advertiser: 10 Apr 1852

Huddersfield Chronicle: 4 Feb 1854

Kendal Mercury: 22 Oct 1836; 15 May 1852; 4 Feb 1854; 29 Apr 1854

Leeds Times: 9 May 1835; 28 Jan 1854

Leicester Chronicle: 28 Jan 1854

Leicestershire Mercury: 28 Jan 1854

Lincolnshire Chronicle: 31 Dec 1841; 11 Mar 1842; 7 Oct 1853; 27 Jan 1854; 3 Feb 1854

Liverpool Daily Post: 29 Nov 1855; 12 Sep 1860

Liverpool Mercury: 22 Oct 1847; 15 Mar 1853; 24 Jun 1853; 23 Sep 1853; 8 Nov 1853; 24 Jan 1854; 31 Jan 1854; 3 Feb 1854; 1 Aug 1861

London Daily News: 26 Jan 1854

London Standard: 24 Jan 1854; 25 Jan 1854; 14 Feb 1854; 21 Dec 1855

Manchester Courier and Lancashire Advertiser: 28 Jan 1854

Manchester Times: 25 Jan 1854; 28 Jan 1854; 8 Feb 1854

Newcastle Guardian and Tyne Mercury: 23 May 1863

Norfolk Chronicle: 11 Feb 1854; 8 Apr 1854

Norfolk News: 4 Mar 1854

North Devon Journal: 16 Mar 1854

North Wales Chronicle: 4 Feb 1854

Portland Guardian and Normanby General Advertiser: 7 Apr 1856

Royal Cornwall Gazette: 27 Jan 1854; 31 Mar 1854

Sheffield Independent: 29 Oct 1853

Stamford Mercury: 17 Sep 1852; 7 Oct 1853; 27 Jan 1854; 3 Feb 1854; 10 Feb 1854; 17 Feb 1854; 10 Mar 1854; 17 Mar 1854; 6 Oct 1854

Stirling Observer: 30 Dec 1852; 13 Oct 1853; 9 Feb 1854; 2 Mar 1854

Sussex Advertiser: 14 Mar 1854

Sydney Morning Herald: 4 May 1854; 25 Jul 1854; 12 Apr 1856; 19 Apr 1856

Taunton Courier and Western Advertiser: 14 Jun 1848; 29 May 1850; 1 Feb 1854

Warrington Guardian: 9 Apr 1853; 8 Oct 1853

Wells Journal: 10 Jul 1852; 29 Apr 1854; 17 Feb 1855

West Kent Guardian: 26 Feb 1853

Western Daily Press: 7 May 1861

Western Times: 22 Oct 1853; 3 Dec 1853; 14 Jan 1854; 28 Jan 1854; 18 Feb 1854; 4 Mar 1854

Westmorland Gazette: 4 Feb 1854; 11 Feb 1854; 25 Mar 1854

Worcestershire Chronicle: 1 Feb 1854

Yorkshire Gazette: 28 Jan 1854

Sources

E.J. Bourke's *Bound for Australia* (2003) is a veritable encyclopaedia of *Tayleur* facts and figures, building on Starkey's *Iron Clipper* (1999), and includes all sorts of technical information, contemporary poems and ballads about the wreck, as well as the clearest passenger and crew list to date. Bourke also quotes from books and reports that I was unable to track down (or couldn't afford to), which was a huge help in establishing the facts of the case. These include the Report to the Right Honourable Lords of the Committee of Privy Council for Trade, (6 Feb 1854), and John Corbett's *The River Irwell* (Abel Heywood and Son, Manchester, 1906).

I searched online so much that my eyesight failed and I needed stronger glasses. Out of the many thousands of pages I browsed, four sites proved crucial to my research:

The British Newspaper Archive (*www.britishnewspaperarchive.co.uk*)
This is a pay-for-use site, which includes scanned newspapers dating back
to the 1700s. It was hugely distracting and entertaining to read the news
as it happened from issue to issue, but also informative. I used it to source
the bulk of my quotes, some of which are from newspapers quoted within
newspapers (the originals not having been scanned yet).

Trove (*http://trove.nla.gov.au*)
This free-to-use Australian site proved essential for tracing ships and the
activities of passengers and crew who had already spent time in Australia
and Tasmania.

Convict records (*www.squidoo.com/convict-ancestor*)
This is another free site with some wonderful images. It takes you through
the procedure for tracing early convicts in Australia and Tasmania step-by-
step.

Ancestry.co.uk (*www.ancestry.co.uk*)
A pay-for-use site, and crucial for access to census records and family trees.
This was usually where I traced *Tayleur* descendants and made contact with
them.

These sites also proved helpful: *www.goldonian.org/barnardo/child_
migrationl.htm* provides a timeline and additional information regarding
child migrants, which was helpful when researching the plight of
impoverished children in the Victorian era. Charles Sale's site *www.
gravestonephotos.com* catalogues gravestone inscriptions and photographs
collected by members of the public, and proved useful for reading faraway
gravestone inscriptions on my laptop.

Glossary of Nautical Terms

Amidships – the middle section of the ship.

Azimuth compass – a compass used in conjunction with the position of the stars or sun and horizon to work out the position of magnetic north.

Belaying pin – club-shaped pin used to bind the sail in place.

Binnacle – case used for holding instruments on the deck of the ship.

Blocks – a flat pulley that ropes run through to increase their mechanical power or keep ends tidy.

Bow – the very front of the ship, the opposite end to the stern.

Bowsprit – the spar sticking out over the water at the very front of the ship.

Branch pilot – sailor who guides ships through channels near a port until they are safely out to sea.

Bulwarks – the built-up sides of the ship.

Clew up – roll up.

Clipper – a sailing ship designed for speed.

Davits – high metal frames used to hang small boats from on board a ship.

Fathom – a unit of length equivalent to 6 feet/1.8 metres.

Forecastle – the upper deck at the front end of the ship, which includes the sailors' living quarters.

Furl up – roll up.

Galley – cooking area.

Hawser – thick rope or cable used for mooring a ship.

Hold – the lower level of the interior of the ship, used to store luggage, cargo, and provisions.

Hull – the watertight outside of the ship.

Jib – triangular sail at the very front of the ship, sometimes also refers to the area near this.

Knot – unit measurement of the speed taken to sail one nautical mile, equivalent to 1.15 miles on land.

Larboard – old term for 'port' or the left side of a ship when facing front.

Leeward/windward – direction the wind is blowing toward.

Maintopsail or *main topsail* – one of the larger sails.

Merchantman – vessel primarily used for transporting goods by the merchant community.

Mizzen topsail – one of the larger sails.

Packet or packet-ship – a ship carrying letters and parcels for the mail service.

Poop – the deck at the rear of the ship that forms a roof over the poop cabin.

Port – the left hand side of the ship if facing the front.

Reef – to reef a sail means to temporarily reduce the area of canvas exposed to the wind.

Sextant – an instrument that allows the user to judge the angle between a celestial object, like the sun or the North Star, and the horizon, so they can calculate approximate locations from charts.

Spanker – the sail situated at the stern or rear of the ship.

Spar – thick wooden pole used to support sails and rigging.

Spritsail-yard – pole on which the spritsail is attached.

Starboard – the right hand side of the ship if facing the front.

Steamer – steamboat.

Stern – the very rear of the ship, the opposite end to the bow.

Tug – tugboat.

Warp – tow-rope.

Known Passengers and Crew on RMS *Tayleur*

T his list of passengers and crew has been compiled using contemporary newspaper reports, survivors' accounts, and E.J. Bourke's 2003 research (which includes brokers' lists of those who booked tickets). There are undoubtedly discrepancies and inaccuracies within this list, due to transcription errors and confusion at the time. I have confirmed 323 men, women, and children as lost in the wreck, yet this still leaves 61 names unaccounted for; their fates remain blank in the list below.

Additionally, there is a discrepancy regarding the number of people to survive the wreck. I have confirmed 297 survivors in the list below, whereas the figure of 282 survivors was agreed upon at the official inquests (based on information provided by the captain and crew, and details recorded on board the *Prince* as the survivors sailed to Dublin). Also, 75 crewmen are listed, although only 70 were named at the inquests. Both figures may be inaccurate, however, as John Aislabie stated at the inquest that a crewman had told him there were 82 crewmen, not 70 as Captain Noble had claimed.

Abrahamson, H (age 32; steerage; survived)
Achan, (age 22; crew; from China; survived)
Adams, M. Anthony R (age 21; crew; from Isle of Man; survived)
Addison, Walker (age 24; steerage/third class; survived)
Affor (age 20; crew; from China; survived)
Aislabie (age 4; second class; from Yorkshire; deceased)
Aislabie John (age 32; second class; upholsterer; from Yorkshire; survived)
Aislabie Mrs (from Yorkshire; deceased)
Alexander, Mrs Elizabeth (from Bridgeton, Glasgow; deceased)
Alexander, John (infant; from Bridgeton, Glasgow; deceased)
Alexander, Peter (from Bridgeton, Glasgow; deceased)
Alexander, Robert (age 29; second class; survived)
Allison, James (age 20; steerage; deceased)
Anatole, V.J./V.C. (age 43; steerage; deceased)
Anderson, Alexander (age 18; steerage)

Anderson, William M (age 24; steerage; deceased)
Andrews, Elizabeth (age 22; steerage; deceased)
Andrews, James (age 24; steerage; deceased)
Andrews, John (infant; steerage; deceased)
Andrews, William (age 28; steerage; deceased)
Angus, David (age 21; steerage; survived)
Anning, H. (age 21; steerage)
Appow (age 25; crew; from China; survived)
Arensberg, F. (second class; survived)
Ashburner, Catherine (age 32; steerage; deceased)
Ashburner, Mary (infant; steerage; deceased)
Ashby, Thomas junior (age 25; from Stamford, Lincolnshire; survived)
Auforth, John (age 19; steerage; deceased)
Auguste, L. (age 45; steerage; deceased)
Aylmer/Almer, John (age 26; crew; from Halifax; survived))
Badcock, William K (age 28; first class; from Bristol; survived)
Bailey, Patrick (age 22; steerage; deceased)
Bailiff, Margaret (age 30; steerage; deceased)
Ball/Barr, John (intermediate or third class; survived)
Barbain/ Barbier, B. (age 28; intermediate; survived)
Barfitt, John R. (age 20; steerage; travelling with John Ryder)
Barrow, Charles (age 27; steerage; survived)
Barton, William (age 29; steerage; survived)
Bayard, (intermediate or steerage; survived)
Beatty, John (age 25; steerage; from Ireland; deceased)
Bell, Joseph (age 33; intermediate; survived)
Ben/Berr, Alexander (third class; survived)
Ben/Berr, John (third class; survived)
Bentz, (steerage; survived)
Berriman/Berryman, James (age 25; intermediate; survived)
Berriman/Berryman, Joseph (age 31; intermediate; survived)
Betts, George (age 19; steerage; from Uffington; deceased)
Bishop, Samuel (age 27; first class or steerage; survived)
Bishop, William (age 20; first class or steerage; survived)
Blair, John (age 24; steerage; from Dundee; deceased)
Blair, Samuel (age 30; steerage; deceased)
Blair, W.J. (age 26; from Doagh, County Antrim; survived)
Boar, Alexander (age 21; steerage; deceased)
Boar, Andrew (age 9; steerage; deceased)
Boar, H. (age 19; steerage; deceased)
Boar, Jane (age 10; steerage; deceased)
Boar, Janet (age 8; steerage; deceased)
Boar, Kate (infant; steerage; deceased)
Boar, M. (age 13; steerage; deceased)
Boar, Margaret (age 3; steerage; deceased)

Boar, Mary (age 28; steerage; deceased)
Boar, R. (age 11; steerage; deceased)
Bourke, Patrick (age 20; steerage; deceased)
Bowden, B. (first class; survived)
Bowden, F. (first class; survived)
Bowden, Francis (age 26; steerage; survived)
Bowden, Samuel (age 20; steerage; survived)
Boyd, Robert (age 25; steerage; from Ballymena, County Antrim; deceased)
Boyd, Timothy (age 19; steerage; from Ballymena, Country Antrim; deceased)
Brayman, H. (second class; survived)
Breen, Daniel (age 17; steerage; deceased)
Bridgman/Bridgeman, Henry (steerage; survived)
Brockman, Samuel (from Falkirk; travelling with McPhersons; survived)
Brook, Gerard (age 20; steerage; deceased)
Brookman, James (age 27; steerage; deceased)
Broomfield, Charles (age 15; steerage; deceased)
Brown, Ann (age 32; steerage; deceased)
Brown, Ann E. (age 22; steerage; deceased)
Brown, James (age 26; crew; from Suffolk; survived)
Brown, James (age 53; steerage; survived)
Browne/Brown, Richard P (age 21; steerage; survived)
Browne/Brown, Thomas (age 51; steerage; survived)
Brugman, H. (second class; survived)
Bryans/Byrons, Edward (age 23; steerage; deceased)
Burban/Burlam, John (age 38; crew; from Cornwall; survived)
Burke, Gerald/Michael (age 28; second class; survived)
Burke, Thomas (crew; survived)
Burne/Burns, E./Francis (intermediate; survived)
Byrne, Michael (intermediate; survived)
Camera, E.S./A. de (age 27; intermediate; survived)
Campbell, D. (age 61; steerage; from Belfast; deceased)
Campbell, Robert (age 22; steerage; from Larne; deceased)
Campbellish, J. (age 22; steerage)
Candari, N. (crew; survived)
Carby, Robert (age 13; intermediate; survived)
Carby, Samuel (age 33; intermediate; survived)
Carby, Sarah Ann (age 37; intermediate; survived)
Carmichael, Duncan (age 11; steerage; from Glasgow; deceased)
Carmichael, Elizabeth (age 16; steerage; from Glasgow; deceased)
Carmichael, Jessie (age 13; steerage; from Glasgow; deceased)
Carmichael, Joseph (age 20; steerage; from Glasgow; deceased)
Carmichael, Joseph (age 50; steerage; from Glasgow; deceased)
Carter, Jonathan (age 24; third class; weaver from Saddleworth, Yorkshire; survived)
Carty, Ann (age 34; third class; survived)
Carty, John (age 30; third class; deceased)

Catham/Cattram, T. (second class; survived)
Cathcart, George (age 19; steerage; from Ireland; deceased)
Cattram/Caltram, Thomas (age 13; steerage; deceased)
Catts, G. (first class; survived)
Chamberlain, G.F. (age 16; intermediate; from Bristol; survived)
Chasey (infant; steerage; from Bristol; deceased)
Chasey, John (age 30; steerage; from Bristol; deceased)
Chasey, Rebecca (age 28; steerage; from Bristol; survived)
Cheriton, F. (age 20; steerage; deceased)
Cherry, Reuben (intermediate; survived)
Chittick, C. (steerage; from Dundee; survived)
Chittick, Charles (age 36; steerage; from Dundee; deceased)
Chittick, Jane/James (age 24; steerage; from Dundee; deceased)
Chittick, Mrs (age 36; steerage; from Dundee; deceased)
Chittick, William (age 30; steerage; from Dundee; deceased)
Clarke, James (age 22; steerage; from Broughshane, County Antrim; deceased)
Clarke, John (age 28; steerage; deceased)
Clarke, William (age 23; steerage)
Clarke/Clark, William (first class; survived)
Clements, William (age 25/26; steerage; deceased)
Clements/Clemenz, VC (age 11; steerage; deceased)
Clofield, James (age 30; steerage; deceased)
Clough, William/John (age 28; family in Manchester; steerage; deceased)
Clough, Mrs (age 30; steerage; from Dundee; deceased)
Clyver, B.F. (age 29; steerage; deceased)
Cock, Jane (age 35; steerage; deceased)
Cock, John (age 34; second class; survived)
Codd, James (passenger; from Dublin; deceased)
Coen/Cohen, Patrick (age 35; steerage; survived)
Coles, John (age 21; steerage; assistant-druggist from Bristol; deceased)
Collins, John (age 28; steerage; survived)
Collins, Joseph (age 29; steerage; deceased)
Collins, W. (steerage; survived)
Comballach/Combillach, Thomas (first class; survived)
Comers, Thomas (age 24; steerage; deceased)
Conner, Thomas (steerage; survived)
Constantine/Considine, Thomas (age 17; steerage; survived)
Cook, William (age 35; crew; from Cornwall; survived)
Coombe, John (age 19; crew; from Bristol)
Coppin, Francis (second class; survived)
Cormick/Cormack, Michael (age 26; steerage; survived)
Cormick/Cormack, Patrick (age 28; steerage; survived)
Cowan, Hugh David (age 19; crew; from Ayrshire; survived)
Cowley/Corley, Alfred/JA (age 26; intermediate; survived)
Crawford, Charles (age 22; steerage; from Larne; deceased)

Crawford, George (steerage; survived)

Creen, T. (steerage; survived)

Crop/Cross, Thomas (age 24; steerage; survived)

Croston, Edwin (infant; steerage; from Liverpool; deceased)

Croston, Mary (age 23; steerage; from Liverpool; deceased)

Croston, Richard (age 21; steerage; carpenter's mate from Liverpool)

Cuddy, William (age 42; steerage or first class; survived)

Cunningham, George F. (age 14 months; from Fife, son of ship surgeon; deceased)

Cunningham, Henry Thomson (age 4; from Fife, son of ship surgeon; deceased)

Cunningham, Robert Hannay Dr (age 27; crew; from Fife; deceased)

Cunningham, Susan Wyse (age 26; from Fife, wife of ship surgeon; deceased)

Curran, M. (age 32; steerage; deceased)

Cutts, George (age 30; first class; from Nottinghamshire; with wife; survived)

Cutts, Martha (age 30; steerage; from Hull; deceased)

Cutts, Patty (first class; from Nottinghamshire; with husband; deceased)

Davidson/Davison, Robert (age 26; steerage; from Broughshane, Country Antrim; deceased)

Davies, Walter (age 42; steerage; deceased)

Davison, Henry (age 33; crew; from Uxbridge)

Davison, Richard (age 26; steerage; cabinet-maker; family in Stockton; deceased)

Davison, Robert (intermediate; from Deal, Kent; survived)

Dawle/Dawe/Dolle, D. (age 25; steerage; deceased)

Dawson, Miss (cabin; with female relatives, from Stockdalewath, Cumbria; deceased)

Dawson, Miss (cabin; with female relatives, from Stockdalewath, Cumbria; deceased)

Dawson, Mrs (cabin; with daughters and sister Miss Penton, from Stockdalewath, Cumbria; deceased)

Dawson, Robert (intermediate; survived)

De Comern, A. (intermediate; survived)

Dennis, William (age 16; crew; from Clovelly, Devon; survived)

Denton, Mary A. (age 26; steerage; deceased)

Diamond, John (steerage; survived)

Dieman, Helen (age 20; steerage; deceased)

Dodd, James (cabin; deceased)

Dolte/Doite, M. (age 23; intermediate; survived)

Downes, George (age 28; second class; survived)

Driscoll, Denis/Dennis (age 25; steerage; survived)

Drummond, John (age 24; steerage)

Drysdale, Pattison (age 28; from Richmond, Surrey; deceased)

Durcault/Durcoult, M. (age 24; steerage or first class; survived)

Durcault/Durcoult, Oneissima (age 22; steerage or first class; survived)

Durcoult/Durcault, Luke (age 22; steerage or first class; survived)

Eberg/Edberg, Ellen (age 25; steerage; deceased)

Eberg/Edberg, Frederick (age 30; steerage; deceased)

Eberg/Edberg, Frederick (infant; steerage; deceased)

Eddy, James (age18; second class; survived)

Elliott, Samuel (age 19; steerage; survived)
Ellis, William (age 20; intermediate; from Ballymena, Country Antrim; deceased)
Fahy, Arthur (age 21; steerage; survived)
Faph/Feight, John (intermediate; survived)
Ferguson, John (age 20; crew; from Kircudbright, Scotland; survived)
Ferguson, William (age 29; steerage; from Manchester; deceased)
Fermy/Ferny/Fermay, Mary (age 24; steerage; deceased)
Fettes/Fetis, Alexander (age 34; second class; survived)
Fettes/Fetis, Margaret (age 4; steerage; deceased)
Fettes/Fetis, Margaret (age 40; steerage; deceased)
Finley, Peter (age 28; intermediate; survived)
Fisher, George (age 26; steerage or first class; survived)
Fitzsimon/Fitzsimons, Henry (age 33; crew; from Whitehaven; survived)
Flamery/Flannery, J. (age 26; steerage; deceased)
Flamery/Flannery, Michael (age 25; steerage)
Fleming, Michael (second class; survived)
Folwell, Edward (age 21; from Bristol; survived)
Forgt, John (age 28; steerage; deceased)
Foy, John (intermediate; survived)
Fraser/Frazer, Alexander (age 23; steerage; survived)
Fraser/Frazer, John (age 49; crew; from Workington, Cumbria; survived)
Frazer/Fraser, Hugh (age 21; steerage; survived)
Fremaine/Framaine, PF (first class; survived)
French, W.J. (age 22; steerage; deceased)
Frengyne/Fuenzyne, P (age 30; steerage; deceased)
Freshwell, Daniel (age 37/10; steerage; deceased)
Freshwell, Thomas (age 10/37; steerage; deceased)
Friend, John (age 21; steerage or third class; survived)
Gamley/Ganly, David (age 20; family in Dublin; deceased)
Garbutt, Martha (age 13; steerage; deceased)
Garnett, George (age 23; steerage; survived)
Gebbie, William (28; steerage; survived)
Geffrey, W. (intermediate; survived)
Gemry, Joseph (age 22; steerage)
George, Nicholas (age 24; crew; from Trieste; survived)
Gibbon/Gibben, Richard (age 40; intermediate; survived)
Gibson, John (age 28; second class; from County Cavan; survived)
Gibson, K. (second class; survived)
Gill, John (intermediate; survived)
Gill, Joseph (age 25; steerage; survived)
Golisarich, Peter (age 20; crew; from Trieste)
Good, William (age 42; steerage; survived)
Gordon, William A. (age 21; second class; survived)
Goulbrough, Charles (age 18; steerage; deceased)
Goulbrough, James (age 21; steerage; deceased)

Goulbrough, John/Joan (age 18; steerage; deceased)
Gourman/Gorman, Thomas (age 40; steerage; deceased)
Gray, John (age 20/26; steerage; deceased)
Gray/Graham, Samuel (age 28; steerage; deceased)
Green, Michael (intermediate; survived)
Green, Thomas (age 22/23; crew or steerage; from Carlisle; deceased)
Greenman, Patrick (age 16; steerage; deceased)
Greenub, John (crew; survived)
Gregory/Grigor, James (age 12; steerage; deceased)
Griffiths, Arthur Charles (infant; steerage; from Herefordshire; survived)
Griffiths, Charles (crew; deceased)
Griffiths, Sarah (age 26; steerage; from Herefordshire; deceased)
Grinell, Michael (first class; survived)
Grundy, John (first class; survived)
Hackney, David (age 21; intermediate; from Doagh, Country Antrim; survived)
Hadley, Mrs (cabin)
Hadley, Samuel (first class; from Cambridge, Gloucestershire; survived)
Hall, Edward (age 24; steerage; survived)
Halzel/Helzel/Holzel, Augusta/Augustus (age 43/40; steerage; deceased)
Haram/Hahn/Herman, Frederick (age 24; steerage; deceased)
Harman/Hardman, George (age 29; steerage)
Harpen/Harper, James (age 16; crew; from Paisley; survived)
Harper, Euphemia (infant; steerage; from Paisley; deceased)
Harper, John (age 13; steerage; from Paisley; deceased)
Harper, John (age 40; steerage; from Paisley; survived)
Harper, Maria (age 5; steerage; from Paisley; deceased)
Harper, Mary (age 9; steerage; from Paisley; deceased)
Harper, Mary Lyons (age 38; steerage; from Paisley; deceased)
Harper, Thomas (crew; survived)
Harper, William (age 3; steerage; from Paisley; deceased)
Harwood, John (age 20; steerage; family in Halberton, Devon)
Hayes, Eliza (age 2; steerage; from Appleton, near Warrington; deceased)
Hayes, Mrs (age 28; steerage; deceased)
Hayes, Mrs (cabin; deceased)
Hegarty, G.W. (age 28; steerage)
Hegarty, J.W. (first class; survived)
Henderson, Alexander (age 12; steerage; deceased)
Henderson, Andrew (age 50; steerage; deceased)
Henderson, George (age 7; steerage; deceased)
Henderson, Isabella (age 30; steerage; deceased)
Henderson, Margaret (age 8; steerage; deceased)
Henderson, Mary (age 11; steerage; deceased)
Henderson, Mrs Ann (age 45; steerage)
Herman (intermediate; survived)
Hesketh, Thomas (age 20; steerage; Liverpool; survived)

Higgen, James A.O. (age 28; steerage; American; survived)

Higgens, John C. (age 21; steerage)

Hinston, Mary (age 22; steerage; deceased)

Hinston, Thomas (age 26; steerage)

Hogarty, J.W. (first class; survived)

Hogg, Ellen (age 55; steerage; deceased)

Hogg, Marion (age 22; steerage; deceased)

Holden, E/Ellen (age 35; steerage; deceased)

Holden, J. (age 49; steerage; deceased)

Holland, Robert (age 33; first class; from Galway; survived)

Hollinax, Edward (age 38; steerage; deceased)

Holt, Daniel (age 24; crew; husband to Sarah; deceased)

Holt, Mrs Sarah E. (age 23; steerage; family in Liverpool; deceased)

Hood, Andrew (age 28; steerage)

Horrell/Horrow, Henry (age 39; steerage; from Devonport; deceased)

Horrell/Horrow, Richard H. (age 9; steerage; travelling with uncle; from Devonport;
   deceased)

Horst, Anne (age 28; steerage; deceased)

Howe, Mark (age 42; steerage; Liverpool; deceased)

Howell, Edward (age 26; steerage)

Hughes, Ellen (age 25; steerage; deceased)

Hughes, George (age 37; steerage; deceased)

Hughes, Richard (age 23; steerage; deceased)

Humphrey/Humphries, George (age 31; crew; from Denbighshire; survived)

Hunt, John F. (crew; Liverpool; survived)

Hunt/Hurst, Michael (age 29; second class; survived)

Huntley, Stephen E. (age 28; steerage; survived)

Irwine/Irvine, Joseph (age 21; crew; Edinburgh; survived)

Isaac, A. (age 28; steerage; deceased)

Jack, Archibald (crew; survived)

Jackson, Albert (second class; survived)

Jaffray, Alfred (age 2; steerage; from Dundee; deceased)

Jaffray, Charles (age 2; steerage; from Dundee; deceased)

Jaffray, Graham (age 10; steerage; from Dundee; deceased)

Jaffray, Jessie/Janet (age 16; steerage; from Dundee; deceased)

Jaffray, John (age 12 ; steerage; from Dundee; deceased)

Jaffray, Margaret (age 8; steerage; from Dundee; deceased)

Jaffray, Mr William (age 35; steerage; spirits dealer from Dundee; deceased)

Jaffray, Mrs Janet (age 35; steerage; from Dundee; deceased)

Jaffray, William (age 17; steerage; apprentice blacksmith from Dundee; survived)

James, John (age 40; steerage; deceased)

James, Thomas (intermediate; survived)

Jenkins, Philip (age 23; steerage; survived)

Jenkins, Samuel (age 32; intermediate; survived)

Jennings, William (from Westwood, Co Cork; deceased)

Johnson, James (age 17; steerage; deceased)
Johnston, Frank (age 18; steerage)
Johnston, John (steerage; survived)
Johnston, Thomas (age 42; steerage; survived)
Johnston/Johnson, Francis (first class; survived)
Johnston/Johnson, Thomas (first class; survived)
Jones, Eliza (age 22; steerage; deceased)
Jones, Ellen (age 18; steerage; deceased)
Jones, Jane (age 20; steerage; deceased)
Jones, John/Henry (crew; from Liverpool; survived)
Jones, Susan (age 24; steerage; deceased)
Jones, Thomas (age 32; steerage)
Jones, William (age 24; from London; survived)
Joseph, B.A. (age 13; steerage; deceased)
Joseph, B.J. (age 42; steerage; deceased)
Joseph, P.C. (age 24; steerage; deceased)
Joseph, P.L. (age 20; steerage; deceased)
Joseph, P.L.C. (infant; steerage; deceased)
Juchler, Albert (age 19; steerage)
Julian, Judge (crew; survived)
Kelly, Robert (age 40; steerage; mason from Whitehaven; deceased)
Kemp, Thomas (age 24; steerage)
Kemp, Thomas (first class; from Stamford, Lincolnshire; survived)
Kerkhouse, Thomas (intermediate; survived)
Kerwin, Andrew (age 21; steerage; from Glan, Co Galway; deceased)
Kerwin, James (age 24; steerage; from Glan, Co Galway; deceased)
Kewley, Edward (age 29; crew; from Whitehaven; deceased)
Keylmack, W. (age 48; steerage; deceased)
Kingsley, William (age 30; steerage; deceased)
Klahershaft/Klatiershaft, B (steerage; survived)
Klattenhoff, B (age 27; steerage; survived)
Klattenhoff, Henry (age 28; steerage; deceased)
Koppin, F (age 29; steerage; deceased)
Koppin, George (age 23; third class; survived)
L'Estrange, Arthur St George (age 27; steerage; family in County Offaly; deceased)
L'Estrange, Mary (age 27; steerage; deceased)
Lamane, August (intermediate; survived)
Larehan, William (steerage; survived)
Lauson/Lansons, R.T. (first class; survived)
Lay, Richard (age 21; steerage)
Lay, Samuel (age 50; steerage)
Leahy, Richard (second class; survived)
Lear, Edward (age 19; steerage)
Lee, Charles Edward (age 19/26; second class; from Tipperary; survived)
Leenehan, Peter/B. (age 28; crew; from Whitehaven; survived)

Leenehan, William (age 31; crew; from Whitehaven; survived)
Legeuet, Peter (age 30; steerage; deceased)
Leggo/Lago, William (age 50; intermediate; survived)
Lenehan, W. (steerage; survived)
Lennan, Joseph M. (crew; survived)
Letio/Letic/Letio, Condic (age 18; steerage; deceased)
Lewis, Edmund (age 35; steerage; deceased)
Lewis, George (age 35; steerage; miner from Merthyr Tydfil; survived)
Lincheon/Lincoln, William (age 18; steerage; deceased)
Lloyd, T. (intermediate; survived)
Lloyd, Thomas (age 26; steerage)
Lloyd, Thomas W (age 48; steerage; deceased)
Lowe, (age 21; from Carron, Falkirk)
Lowe, (age 50; from Carron, Falkirk)
Lumane, August (intermediate; survived)
Lunt, David (age 7/28; steerage; deceased)
Lunt, Elizabeth/Patrick (age 35/33; steerage; deceased)
Lunt, Thomas/Joseph (age 28/7; steerage; deceased)
Lurcombe/Luscom/Luscam, John (age 23; second class; survived)
Lynch, Pat (age 21; steerage; from Lurcombe, Dartmoor)
Lyons, Alexander (steerage; survived)
Lyons, A.W. (age 84; steerage)
Lyson, Joseph (age 28; steerage)
MacGill, Mary (age 25; steerage; travelling with cousin John Beattie and James
   Montford from Broughshane, Ireland; deceased)
Maclean, Archibald (age 28; crew; survived)
MacMahon, Patrick (age 26; steerage)
Magee, A. (steerage; survived)
Marberg, H. (age 30; steerage; deceased)
Marberg, Mrs (age 28; steerage; deceased)
Mario/Marion/Merion, James (age 23; intermediate; survived)
Marromatti/Maromatil, John (age 23; crew; from the Ionian Isles; survived)
Martin, John (crew; survived)
Matthews, Mr (age 23; steerage)
Matthews/Mathews, M. (third class; survived)
Maxwell, Charles (age 31; crew; from Liverpool; survived)
Mayman, John (age 18; steerage; cotton-weaver from Dukinfield; deceased)
McBride, George (age 25; steerage; from Ballymena. County Antrim; survived)
McCarthy, William (age 24; steerage; from Ballymena, County Antrim; survived)
McCullough/McCullagh, Eliza (age 22; steerage; from Ireland; deceased)
McDonald, William (age 21; steerage; from Lurgan; deceased)
McGee, A. (age 35; steerage; survived)
McGrath, John (age 36; steerage; survived)
McGuire, C. (age 23; steerage; survived)
McKay, James (age 20; steerage; survived)

McKay, Joseph (age 28; steerage; survived)

McKenzie, Fanny (age 25; steerage; from Belfast; deceased)

McKenzie, John (age 48; steerage; from Belfast; deceased)

McKenzie, Mary (age 15; steerage; from Belfast; deceased)

McKenzie, Mary (age 46; steerage; deceased)

McKenzie, Matilda (age 24; steerage; from Belfast; deceased)

McKenzie, Peter (age 28; steerage; deceased)

McKittock, William (age 21; steerage; from Ballymena; deceased)

McLellan, James (age 26; crew; from Canada; survived)

McLetchie, J. (age 28; steerage; deceased)

McMahon, Patrick (steerage; survived)

McMickin, John (age 24; steerage; from Doagh, County Antrim; deceased)

McNaughton, F./P. (age 20; steerage; deceased)

McNaughton/McNaughten, John (first class; survived)

McPherson, Agnes (age 2 ½; steerage; Falkirk; deceased)

McPherson, John (age 31; steerage; Falkirk; deceased)

McPherson, Thomasina (age 21; steerage; travelling from Falkirk with Samuel Brockman, brother, and husband and daughter; deceased)

McWey/McVey, M. (age 17; steerage; deceased)

McWhirr/McWhinny, John (age 33; steerage; deceased)

Mearn/Mear/Mears, Thomas (third class; survived)

Merton, James (age 22; steerage)

Middleton, Mrs (age 26; steerage; deceased)

Middleton, Robert (age 28; steerage; deceased)

Miller, Anne (age 27; steerage; Glasgow; deceased)

Miller, Ellen (infant; steerage; Glasgow; deceased)

Miller, Giles/Hugh (37; steerage; from Broughshane, County Antrim; deceased)

Miller, James (age 13; steerage; deceased)

Miller, James (age 20; second class; from Broughshane, County Antrim; deceased)

Miller, James (age 31/38; steerage; deceased)

Miller, Margaret (age 18; steerage; from Broughshane, County Antrim; deceased)

Miller, Thomas (age 8; steerage; deceased)

Miller, William (age 11; steerage; deceased)

Mitchell, A Rose/Rosse (age 23; crew; from Trieste; survived)

Mitchell, James (age 21; steerage; deceased)

Mitchell, Jane (age 50; steerage; Aberdeen; deceased)

Mitchell, Thomas (age 35; steerage; deceased)

Mollar, H (age 19; steerage)

Montgomery, J (age 28; steerage; deceased)

Moody, Thomas (age 28; steerage; survived)

Moore, Catherine (age 20; steerage; from Broughshane, County Antrim; deceased)

Moore, James (infant; steerage; from Broughshane, County Antrim; deceased)

Moore, Samuel (age 45; steerage; from Broughshane, County Antrim; deceased)

Moran, Charles (age 26; steerage; deceased)

Moran, John (age 24; steerage; deceased)

Morgan, Daniel (age 34; steerage; deceased)

Morgan, John (age 21; steerage; deceased)

Morien/Morio, A. (age 30; steerage; survived)

Morrison, Isaac (age 25; steerage; from Ballymena, County Antrim; deceased)

Morrison, Robert (age 12; steerage)

Mountford/Moutford/Montford, James (age 23; steerage; from Ballymena, County Antrim; survived)

Murphy, Michael (crew; from Wexford, Ireland; survived)

Nicholas, Antonia (age 22; crew; from Trieste; survived)

Nicholl, William (age 25; steerage; deceased)

Nicholls/Nichols, John (age 48; steerage; from Cawsand Bay, Devonshire; survived)

Nicholson, Robert David (age 26; steerage; from Fife; deceased)

Noble, John (age 27; crew; survived)

O'Brien, John (age 25; steerage; survived)

O'Brien, Julia (age 33; steerage; deceased)

O'Connor, James M. (age 22; steerage; deceased)

O'Higgins, Patrick (American; survived)

O'Keefe, Mrs (from Ballyvartella, Co Tipperary; deceased)

O'Reilly, Madeline (age 13; steerage; deceased)

Oldfield, James (steerage; survived)

Oliver, Betsy (age 30; steerage; deceased)

Oliver, Charlotte (age 11; steerage; deceased)

Oliver, George (age 32; steerage; tailor from Devonport; deceased)

Oliver, Louisa (age 6; steerage; deceased)

Organ, James (age 23; steerage; survived)

Ormsberg, Francis (second class; survived)

Oufferht, John (second class; survived)

Palmer, Mrs (age 28/26; steerage; from Broughty Ferry, Dundee; deceased)

Park, Thomas (age 23; crew; Carlisle)

Parry, William (age 33; crew; London)

Patton/Patten, William (age 23; steerage; from Lurgan, County Armagh; deceased)

Pearson, Robert (age 26; steerage)

Pearson, Thomas (age 23; steerage; deceased)

Peat, Ann (age 28/22; steerage; deceased)

Penard/Perrard (intermediate; survived)

Penton, Miss (age 23; cabin; travelling with her sister, Mrs Dawson, and two nieces, from Stockdalewath, Cumbria; deceased)

Perry, Daniel (age 28; steerage)

Peser, John (age 38; crew; from Bombay)

Peterson, Ernest/Ernst (age 24; steerage)

Pheff/Phaff, Joseph (age 23/22; steerage; deceased)

Phillips, John (age 22; second class or steerage; survived)

Phillips, William (age 33; second class or steerage; survived)

Pierce ('elderly'; deceased)

Pole (age 30/80; first class; butcher from Bristol; survived)

Pope, Francis (age 15; steerage)
Pope, John (age 40; steerage)
Popham, James (age 29; third class; survived)
Porter, James (age 23; steerage)
Porter, John (first cousin of William; from Meath; survived)
Porter, Joseph
Porter, William (first cousin of John; from Meath; survived)
Postlethwaite, Jane (age 6; steerage; deceased)
Postlethwaite, Martha (age 28; steerage; deceased)
Postlethwaite, Martha (infant; steerage; deceased)
Postlethwaite, Sarah (age 32; steerage; deceased)
Postlethwaite, Thomas (age 36; steerage; deceased)
Postlethwaite, Thomas (age 8; steerage; deceased)
Prairam, S. (crew; survived)
Prard, Seymour (crew; from Bombay; survived)
Pratt, E/David (crew; from Cellardyke, Fife; survived)
Price, Charles (age 48; steerage; deceased)
Price, William (age 33; steerage)
Prockman, S. (intermediate; survived)
Pyle, Charles (age 18; steerage; deceased)
Raleigh/ Rawley James (age 19; steerage; survived)
Ray, W. (crew; survived)
Rear, Thomas (age 33; steerage; deceased)
Reed, Peter (crew; survived)
Regman, Henry (age 23; steerage; deceased)
Reidy, Michael (age 28; second class; from Scariff, County Galway; survived)
Rendell/Rendall, W/John (age 24; crew; from Worcestershire; survived)
Rice, John (crew; survived)
Richards, John (age 28; crew; from Exmouth)
Richmond, James (age 20; steerage; survived)
Riley, Susan (age 32; steerage; deceased)
Riley, William (age 33; steerage; deceased)
Rimes, Betsy (age 28; steerage; from Ailsworth, Northamptonshire; deceased)
Rimes, Ellen Ann (age 4; steerage; from Ailsworth, Northamptonshire; survived)
Rimes, Gabriel (age 30; steerage; farmer from Ailsworth, Northamptonshire; survived)
Roberts, F.J. (crew; survived)
Roberts, John (age 19; crew; from Liverpool; survived)
Roberts, Thomas (age 28; crew; from Elsinore, Denmark; survived)
Robinson, John F. (age 21; first class or steerage; farrier from Neston, Cheshire; survived)
Rolando, Demetri (crew; survived)
Ross/Rose, Andrew (age 5; steerage; deceased)
Ross/Rose, Barbara (age 16; steerage; deceased)
Ross/Rose, Donald (age 7; steerage; deceased)
Ross/Rose, George (age 44; steerage; deceased)

Ross/Rose, Grace (age 9; steerage; deceased)
Ross/Rose, Isabella (age 2; steerage; deceased)
Ross/Rose, John (age 14; steerage; deceased)
RossRose, Mrs (age 43; steerage; deceased)
Rowden/Rowley, B./James (age 20; steerage; survived)
Rowe, Ambrose (age 43; steerage; deceased)
Rowland, T./Owen (age 26; crew; from Holyhead; survived)
Ryan, Con (age 45; steerage; survived)
Ryan, Michael (age 50; steerage; deceased)
Ryder, Richard (age 19; intermediate; survived)
Ryder/Rider, John (age 21; intermediate; travelling with John Barfitt; survived)
Ryder/Rider, William (age 42/43; intermediate; survived)
Sambells, Francis (age 23; steerage; deceased)
Sambells, Mary (age 25; steerage; deceased)
Saunderson/Sanderson, John (age 22; crew; from Maryport, Cumbria; survived)
Sawdry/Sawdy/Sandy, William (age 26; steerage; survived)
Schul/Sheil, Robert (age 26; steerage)
Scott, William (age 27; crew)
Scott/See, William (age 23; second class; survived)
Searson, Robert (from Market Deeping, Lincolnshire; deceased)
Shan, James (age 21; steerage)
Shaw, F.J./James (age 33; intermediate; from Broughshane, County Antrim; survived)
Shaw/Shae, F.S. (second class; survived)
Shepphard, Elizabeth (nurse of ship surgeon's children; deceased)
Sheridan, Richard (first class; survived)
Sheridan, W.D./William Henry (age 43; crew; from North Shields; survived)
Shewell/Sheil, R. (steerage; from Lurgan, County Armagh; survived)
Sjellgan/Slellgan, D. (age 23; steerage; deceased)
Skelzig, William (age 38; crew; from Ryton, County Durham; survived)
Sleyerty/Stenhart/Stehardt/Stelhardt, Lorenzo (age 33; intermediate)
Sloan, Hamilton (age 23; intermediate; from Broughshane, County Antrim; survived)
Smeril, R (third class; survived)
Smith, John (age 8; steerage; deceased)
Smith, Joseph/Joshua 26; second class; survived)
Smith, Margaret (age 38; steerage; deceased)
Spencer/Spenser/Sponser, William (age 26; second class; survived)
Stanlake, Mary (age 27; steerage; deceased)
Stanlake, Mary (age 62; steerage; deceased)
Stanlake, Samuel (age 62; steerage; deceased)
Stanlake, Susan (age 19; steerage; deceased)
Starman, William (second class; survived)
Stodhart/Stodhardt/Stodgarts, James (age 35; survived)
Stott, Sarah (age 26; deceased)
Stott, Thomas (age 29; deceased)
Surril/Smyrt/Smarit/Surri/Suru, RJ (age 26; steerage; from Belfast; survived)

Sutton, Daniel (age 53; steerage; deceased)
Sutton, Jane (age 23; steerage; deceased)
Sutton, John (age 19; steerage; deceased)
Swan, John (age 24; intermediate; survived)
Swift, Mary (age 47; steerage; deceased)
Swift, Mary E. (age 14; steerage; deceased)
Swift, Thomas (age 22; steerage; deceased)
Swift, William/J. (age 20; steerage; survived)
Symonds, William (age 20; steerage; deceased)
Taylor, Thomas (age 20; first class or steerage; survived)
Taylor, William (age 33; crew; from Accrington, Lancashire; survived)
Tebbutt/Tibbutt, Thomas (age 26; steerage; from Stamford, Lincolnshire; survived)
Tew, Edward (age 21; second class; from Wakefield, Yorkshire; survived)
Thain, John (age 11 months; steerage; from Elgin; deceased)
Thain, Mrs Margaret (age 30; steerage; from Elgin; deceased)
Thain, Peter (age 24; steerage; baker from Elgin; deceased)
Theacker, Henry (age 13; steerage; deceased)
Thomas, Alexander (age 27; first class or steerage; survived)
Thomas, Henry (age 38/36; steerage; deceased)
Thomas, John (age 48; first, second, or third class; survived)
Thomas, Samuel (age 48; intermediate; survived)
Thomas, William (age 36; third class; survived)
Thompson, James (age 23; second class; survived)
Thompson, John (age 22; steerage; survived)
Thompson, Mr (cabin)
Thompson, R (age 40; steerage; from Ohio; survived)
Thompson, William (saloon; from Liverpool; survived)
Tiberton, Thomas (first class; survived)
Titles/Titiss, Alexander (second class; survived)
Tobin, James (age 20; intermediate; survived)
Todhunter, Joseph (age 27; second class; survived)
Town, John (age 19; steerage; deceased)
Town, William (age 42; steerage; deceased)
Toy, Samuel Tough (first class; survived)
Tracy, T./Y./Timothy (age 18/13; steerage; deceased)
Trumbell/Trumble, William (age 42; crew; from Liverpool; survived)
Turner, Isaac (age 33; steerage)
Turner, W. (second class; survived)
Twill, Thomas (intermediate; survived)
Unknown black seaman (survived)
Virgoz (second class; survived)
Vivers, William (age 22; intermediate; from Dumfries; survived)
Vonbourg/Von Burg/Voubourg (intermediate; survived)
Vont, John (second class; survived)
Wales, William (age 22; crew; from Kirkdale, Liverpool; survived)

Walker, James (age 24; steerage; from Belfast; survived)
Wallace, H. (crew; survived)
Wallis, Elward/Edward (crew; survived)
Walsey, George (age 18; steerage)
Ward, Thomas (age 22; first class; survived)
Wardlaw, Catherine (age 27; steerage; deceased)
Wardlaw, James (age 37; steerage; deceased)
Warren, James (age 20; steerage; survived)
Watson, B (age 25; second class; mason from Cellardyke, Fife; survived)
Watson, James/John (age 20; steerage; survived)
Watson, Thomas (age 23; steerage)
Wayer, F. (age 36; steerage; deceased)
Wearn/Wearne, Richard (age 24; first class or steerage; survived)
Wearn/Wearne/Wearon, Joseph (age 26; first class or steerage; survived)
Webb, H. (age 13/18; steerage; deceased)
Webster, Catherine (age 23; steerage; from Stamford, Lincolnshire; deceased)
West, John (age 34; crew; from Harwich, Essex; survived)
Wetyle/Wetyte, A. (first class; survived)
White, Honora (cabin; deceased)
White, Mrs (cabin; deceased)
White, Richard (cabin; deceased)
Whitmarsh/Whitemarsh/Whitmush, James (age 29; intermediate; survived)
Whittall, Thomas (age 42; steerage; deceased)
Wild, Elizabeth Ann (age 20; steerage; deceased)
Willet, Thomas (steerage; porter from Manchester; survived)
Williams, E.H. (age 28; steerage; assistant chemist from Bristol; deceased)
Williams, James (age 33; intermediate; survived)
Williams, John (age 20; crew; from Liverpool; survived)
Williams, Joshua (age 24; crew; from Trieste)
Wills, Esther (age 27; steerage; deceased)
Wilson, David M. (age 25; steerage; deceased)
Wilson, Donald Ross (age 24/19; family in Glasgow and Inverness; deceased)
Wilson, J./Thomas (second class; mason from Fife; survived)
Wilson, James Waters (age 22/21; family in Glasgow and Inverness; deceased)
Wilson, John Ross (age 18/23; family in Glasgow and Inverness; deceased)
Wizenbach, C. (age 33; steerage; deceased)
Wolechewick, Peter (crew; survived)
Wood, James (age 31; weaver from Delph, Yorkshire; deceased)
Workhouse/Wora, Thomas (age 41; steerage; deceased)
Worm/Worms, James (intermediate; survived)
Wright, David (age 38; steerage; deceased)
Wright, Thomas (age 40; steerage; deceased)
Yates/Yeates, George (age 29; intermediate; survived)
Yeo, Richard (second class; survived)

Index

Discover Your History

Ancestors • Heritage • Memories

Each issue of *Discover Your History* presents special features and regular articles on a huge variety of topics about our social history and heritage – such as our ancestors, childhood memories, military history, British culinary traditions, transport history, our rural and industrial past, health, houses, fashions, pastimes and leisure ... and much more.

Historic pictures show how we and our ancestors have lived and the changing shape of our towns, villages and landscape in Britain and beyond.

Special tips and links help you discover more about researching family and local history. Spotlights on fascinating museums, history blogs and history societies also offer plenty of scope to become more involved.

Keep up to date with news and events that celebrate our history, and reviews of the latest books and media releases.

Discover Your History presents aspects of the past partly through the eyes and voices of those who were there.

FREE BOOK WHEN YOU SUBSCRIBE TO *Discover Your History*

UK only

Discover Your History is in all good newsagents and also available on subscription for six or twelve issues. For more details on how to take out a subscription and how to choose your free book, call 01778 392013 or visit **www.discoveryourhistory.net**

www.discoveryourhistory.net